CHRISSY FREER

supergrains

CHRISSY FREER

supergrains

cook your way to great health

appetite

by RANDOM HOUSE

Contents

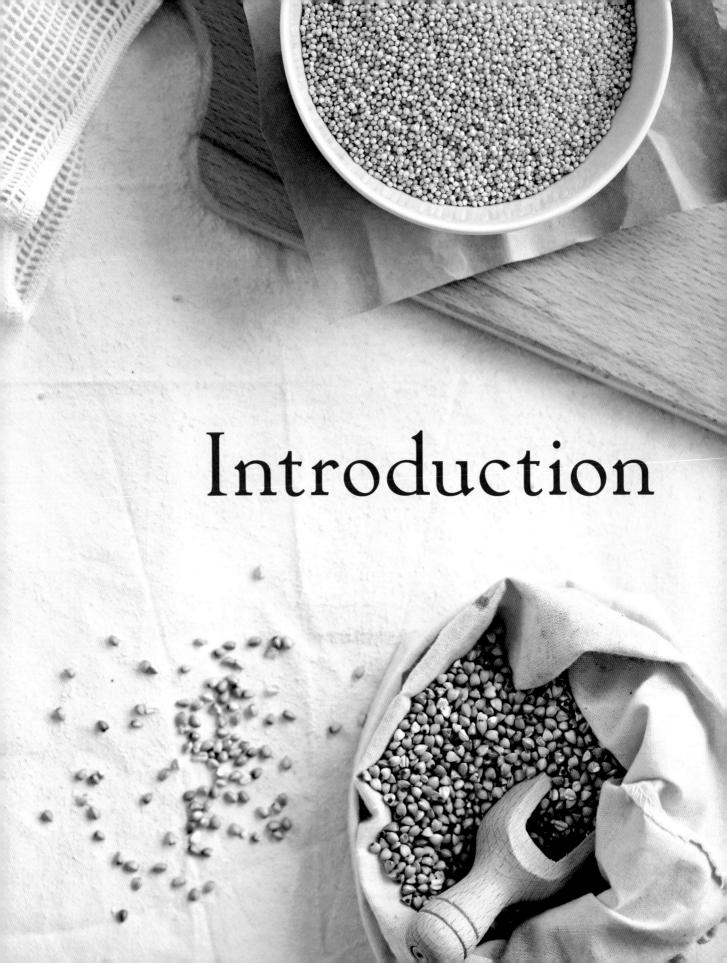

Introduction

What are supergrains?

In today's society, the impact food can have on our health is becoming increasingly important. A superfood is a food that by nature is nutrient dense compared to its energy value. Supergrains are grains that are not only packed with nutrients, but have also been linked to many health benefits, which is why they are currently gaining worldwide interest.

Let's start by defining grains. These are the seeds of certain plants, where the hard inedible husk or outer layer is removed, leaving the edible grain (or berry). Unrefined (whole) grains contain all three parts of the grain: the bran, germ and endosperm. Supergrains (in their simplest forms) are all unrefined grains. Refined grains have the bran and germ removed, leaving just the endosperm which contains the least vitamins and minerals.

This book explores 12 supergrains: quinoa, amaranth, buckwheat, brown rice, chia, millet, oats, spelt, kamut, barley, farro and freekeh. We look at their history, nutritive and health benefits, what they are best used for and how to cook them. There are delicious recipes for each supergrain so you will have the confidence to incorporate them into your everyday life.

Although some of the supergrains are quite common, others you may not have heard of, despite the fact that they have been around for centuries. Spelt, for instance, was a staple grain in ancient civilizations such as Greece and Rome. One of the main reasons for their decline in popularity was the modernization of farming methods, which produced more refined, highly processed foods. Compared to these new, refined foods, supergrains came to be considered by many cultures as peasant food, only eaten by the very poor or even fed to the animals.

The problem with replacing supergrains with refined grains, however, is that the latter are much lower in nutrients, healthy fats, antioxidants and phytonutrients. Although most of the grains currently consumed in first-world countries are highly refined, such as white rice, white wheat flour and ground cornmeal, there is renewed interest in supergrains for their health benefits, superior taste and suitability for restricted diets, such as gluten and wheat intolerances, vegetarians and vegans.

Another reason for the re-emergence of supergrains is a growing interest in making food more 'simplistic', by going back to its original source and subjecting it to minimal refining. Farmers' markets, the organic and biodynamic food movements, the demand for quality ingredients and the move towards 'whole' foods all indicate an increasing awareness and interest in what goes into food products and their natural health benefits.

As supergrains gain in popularity, their availability also improves. Quinoa, for example, was once considered a 'speciality' grain, only found in serious health food stores and on restaurant menus, but today it can be found in almost every major supermarket. Kamut and spelt are enjoying a renewed popularity, too, especially in the form of baked products such as bread. Chia is also receiving a lot of attention as it contains more omega 3 and dietary fiber than any other natural food.

The recipes in this book reflect my approach to health and eating — everything in moderation, with a focus on whole foods, such as supergrains. Eating responsible portion sizes means that occasional treats can be enjoyed (and, in fact, are a must!). Meals should be balanced, with one portion of protein, one portion of complex carbohydrates and two to three servings of vegetables. I hope these delicious recipes inspire you and contribute to your own healthy eating.

Health benefits

Controlling blood sugar levels

The glycemic index (GI) is a measure of the speed with which individual carbohydrate foods are converted into blood sugar. The lower the GI of a food, the slower it releases glucose, resulting in sustained energy. High-GI foods, on the contrary, release glucose quickly and give a spike in blood sugar. As supergrains are complex carbohydrates, they generally have a low GI, providing slowly released energy that is extremely beneficial for everyone, particularly those with diabetes.

High fiber

Supergrains are an excellent source of dietary fiber, whether soluble, insoluble or both. Soluble fiber is water soluble, as the name suggests, and forms a thick gel-like substance. This gel helps keep the bowel healthy, reduces blood cholesterol and slows the release of sugars in the blood, which is very useful for those with diabetes. Insoluble fiber, on the other hand, stays intact even when in contact with water. Insoluble fiber helps in preventing constipation and irritable bowel syndrome, keeps your colon healthy and assists with heart health.

Reduced risk of obesity/weight management

Studies are beginning to show that supergrains can play an important role in reducing the risk of obesity when they are used as a tool for weight control. They are higher in fiber than highly processed grains, especially soluble fiber which can increase satiety so you feel full for longer and therefore eat less overall.

Prebiotic effect

Prebiotics are foods that stimulate the growth of healthy bacteria, helping to produce digestive enzymes. There have been recent studies on the prebiotic effects that supergrains can have in the digestive system, mainly due to the fermentation of the soluble fibre they contain.

Reduced risk of cardiovascular disease

The relationship between the consumption of supergrains and the reduced risk of cardiovascular disease is of great interest. Supergrains that are high in soluble fiber (such as oats and barley) have been proven to be effective in reducing blood cholesterol. Supergrains are also associated with a reduced risk of stroke, healthier carotid arteries and reduced blood pressure.

Reduced risk of certain cancers

Supergrains contain many natural compounds that protect cells from damage and therefore may reduce the risk of certain cancers. Insoluble fiber, in particular, is thought to reduce the risk of colon cancer by maintaining a healthy colon. Other compounds to be of benefit include antioxidants, phenols, lignans and saponins.

Gluten free

Supergrains can play an important role in the diets of people who are celiac or gluten intolerant. Quinoa, amaranth, buckwheat, brown rice, chia and millet do not contain any gluten. Many recipes in this book are suitable for those following a gluten-free diet and others can be adjusted slightly to become completely gluten free.

Cooking guide

Grain	Per 1 cup raw weight	Quantity of liquid required	Cooking time	Description	Yield (approx.)
Quinoa	7 oz	2 cups	12 minutes	Absorption method, grains turn translucent and uncurl, and have an *al dente* texture	3 cups
Amaranth	7$\frac{1}{2}$ oz	2$\frac{1}{2}$ cups	20 minutes	Absorption method, grains become *al dente* with a slightly sticky texture	2$\frac{1}{2}$ cups
Buckwheat	7 oz	2 cups	10–12 minutes	Gentle boil, grains swell and keep some texture	3 cups
Brown rice	7 oz	1$\frac{1}{2}$ cups (absorption) 6 cups (gentle boil)	25–30 minutes	Gentle boil or absorption method, grains swell and have a slightly chewy texture	3 cups
Millet (hulled)	7$\frac{1}{2}$ oz	2–2$\frac{1}{2}$ cups	20 minutes	Absorption method, grains tend to stick together slightly and then separate on cooling, and have an *al dente* texture	3$\frac{1}{2}$ cups
Oats (rolled)	3$\frac{1}{4}$ oz	2 cups	5–10 minutes	Absorption method, results in a creamy, soft porridge	2 cups
Spelt	7 oz	6–8 cups	45–50 minutes	Gentle boil, grains swell and have a slightly chewy texture	2$\frac{1}{2}$ cups
Kamut	7 oz	6–8 cups	45–50 minutes	Gentle boil, grains swell and have a slightly chewy texture	2$\frac{1}{2}$ cups
Pearl barley	7 oz	6 cups	30 minutes	Gentle boil, grains swell and have a slightly chewy texture	3$\frac{1}{2}$ cups
Farro (cracked)	6 oz	6–8 cups	15–20 minutes	Gentle boil, grains swell and keep some texture	2$\frac{1}{2}$ cups
Freekeh (whole grain)	7 oz	6–8 cups	45–50 minutes	Gentle boil, grains swell and have a slightly chewy texture	2$\frac{1}{2}$ cups

How to use supergrains

Grain	Flavor characteristics	Goes well with ...	Use in ...	Gluten free
Quinoa	Mild, nutty, slightly bitter	Extremely versatile. Great with Middle Eastern spices, Mediterranean flavors, fresh herbs, citrus and even Asian flavors	Salads, pilafs, stuffings for meat or vegetables, soups, stews, porridge and desserts	✓
Amaranth	Herbaceous, grassy, sticky	Nuts, honey, chocolate and cinnamon, and Mexican flavors such as chile, paprika and corn	Porridge, salads, soups and stews (when combined with other grains)	✓
Buckwheat	Earthy, dark, slightly meaty	Foods that have natural sweetness and/or saltiness such as miso, roast beet, seafood and mushrooms, as well as creamy foods	Salads, risotto, pilafs, soups and granola. Flour is used in pancakes and other baked goods	✓
Brown rice	Nutty, slightly sweet, chewy	Other foods with nuttiness, saltiness or natural sweetness such as roasted vegetables, dried fruit and nuts, feta cheese and Asian flavors	Salads, risotto, pilafs, stuffings for meat or vegetables, stir-fries and rice dessert	✓
Chia	Neutral, mild	Provides texture and will team well with almost anything, sweet or savory. Delicious combined with oats, nuts, seeds, dried fruit and chocolate	Smoothies, dressings, baked goods and sprinkle over salads	✓
Millet	Buttery, corn-like, mellow	Cheeses such as Parmesan and feta, fresh herbs, corn, citrus and berries	Salads, pilafs, stuffings, porridge, soups, stews, desserts and to make a polenta-like dish	✓
Oats	Creamy, slightly sweet, toasty	Cheese, nuts, chocolate, brown sugar and milk	Granola, porridge, baked goods and coatings (instead of bread crumbs)	
Spelt	Nutty, slightly earthy, chewy	Nuts, dried fruit and chocolate, and Mediterranean flavors such as basil, olives, tomato, cheese and eggplant	Salads, pilafs and stuffings for meat or vegetables. Flour is used in bread, pasta, baked goods and desserts	
Kamut	Buttery, nutty	Foods that are naturally slightly sweet or nutty, such as roasted vegetables and pine nuts	Salads, pilafs and stuffings for meat or vegetables. Flour is used in bread, pasta and baked goods	
Pearl barley	Nutty, slightly chewy	Very versatile. Perfect with stronger flavors such as lamb, mushrooms, soy and miso	Salads, risotto, pilafs, stuffings, soups, stews and sweet desserts	
Farro (cracked)	Nutty, mild, slightly chewy	Ideal with Italian flavors such as pancetta, herbs, Parmesan and red wine	Salads, pilafs, risotto, stuffings, soups, stews and pasta	
Freekeh (whole grain)	Nutty, slightly herbaceous, green	Can take on quite robust flavors, such as cumin, paprika, pomegranate, lamb and mint	Salads, pilafs, stuffings for meat or vegetables, soups and stews	

Quinoa

NUTRITIONAL INFORMATION
(per 7 oz/1 cup cooked quinoa)

Energy: 929 kilojoules, 222 calories Protein: 8.1 g Total fat: 3.6 g

Saturated fat: 0 g Carbohydrate: 39.4 g Sugars: 0 g Dietary fiber: 5.2 g

Cholesterol: 0 mg Folate: 77.7 µg Iron: 2.8 mg Magnesium: 118 mg

Manganese: 1.2 mg Phosphorus: 281 mg Sodium: 13 mg

Gluten free

Quinoa

Quinoa (pronounced keen-wah) is an ancient grain of the Andes mountain range in South America, and was once the staple food of the Incas. It is enjoying a resurgence in popularity, and has gained recognition as a 'supergrain' due to its high levels of protein, balanced essential amino acid profile, rich nutrient content and gluten-free qualities. Its ease of preparation and versatility also make it stand out from some of the other grains.

Although it's considered and called a grain, quinoa is in fact a pseudo-grain, being the seed of a leafy plant distantly related to spinach, called *Chenopodium quinoa* (also known as goosefoot). Its history dates back some 5000 years, when it was second only to potatoes as a staple food of the Incas, who called it the 'mother seed'. They considered it sacred and believed it increased stamina, so their warriors ate it to keep them strong.

Today, quinoa has had a massive resurgence, as its unique nutritional qualities have been rediscovered. Quinoa is naturally gluten and wheat free, making it gentle on digestion and suitable for the ever-increasing number of people following a gluten-free diet. It is also an amazing food for vegetarians and vegans, not only because it is a rich source of protein, but also due to its balanced essential amino acid profile. It contains all the essential amino acids, making it a rare complete vegetable protein source. Of particular note is lysine, an amino acid that assists in tissue repair and growth.

In addition to protein, quinoa is rich in many nutrients, such as dietary fiber, and it is linked to reducing the risk of cardiovascular disease, certain cancers and type 2 diabetes. It is also high in manganese and is a good source of phosphorus, magnesium and folate.

Quinoa is available in various forms: as a whole grain, flakes and, less commonly, flour. Quinoa grains look like tiny flat disks. As the grain cooks the center seed becomes translucent and soft, while the outside germ separates from the seed and looks like a white ring that retains an *al dente* texture. The grain can be found in various colors, but white, red or black are the most common. The red and black varieties have a slightly firmer texture once cooked and are a little stronger in flavor than the white variety.

One of the main attractions of quinoa is how easy and quick it is to cook. It does not require presoaking or toasting, and is ready in just 12 minutes. The grain is fabulous used in salads, as you would use rice, couscous or pasta. It can also be used to stuff vegetables and meat or added to soups, stews and curries, pilafs and more.

Quinoa flakes are even quicker to prepare, and can be used to make a delicious gluten-free porridge. They are fantastic added to baked goods such as muffins, breads and cookies, and make a crisp and golden coating when used as a substitute for bread crumbs. Quinoa flour is harder to find, but it can be used in gluten-free baking, such as cakes and breads, or to make pasta. It does tend to have a slightly bitter taste, so is best combined with ingredients that have some natural sweetness.

To cook quinoa

Most of the quinoa available today has been pre-rinsed to remove the bitter 'saponin' coating around the grain, and therefore it only requires a brief rinse before cooking.

Put the quinoa in a sieve and rinse for 30 seconds under cold running water. For every 200 g (7 oz/1 cup) of grain, add 500 ml (17 fl oz/2 cups) water, then bring to a boil over medium heat. Cover, reduce the heat to low and simmer for 12 minutes or until the water has evaporated and the grains are tender. (The red and black varieties of the grain may need a few extra minutes of cooking.) Remove from the heat and set aside to cool.

NOTE For a slightly nuttier flavor, toast the quinoa in a hot dry pan for 1–2 minutes, stirring, prior to cooking.

Breakfast quinoa with vanilla roasted plums

PREPARATION TIME: 10 MINUTES

COOKING TIME: 10 MINUTES

SERVES 4

8 (about 1 lb) firm ripe plums, stones removed and cut into quarters

3 tablespoons sugar

1 teaspoon vanilla bean paste

1 teaspoon lemon juice

1⅓ cups quinoa flakes

1 cup milk

½ teaspoon ground cinnamon

1 Preheat the oven to 350°F. Put the plums in a medium bowl, add the sugar, vanilla and lemon juice and toss to coat. Place the plums, cut side up, in a roasting pan and bake for 10 minutes or until tender. (The cooking time will vary depending on the ripeness of the plums.)

2 Meanwhile, put the quinoa flakes, milk, cinnamon and 2 cups water in a large saucepan. Cook, stirring, over medium heat for 3–4 minutes or until thick and creamy.

3 Divide the quinoa porridge among 4 bowls, top with some roasted plums and spoon over any pan juices.

* *Quinoa flakes make a fantastic gluten-free porridge that only takes minutes to cook and is packed with protein and carbohydrates. It's the perfect way to start the day and will keep you feeling full for a long time.*

Banana, honey & walnut bread

PREPARATION TIME: 20 MINUTES
COOKING TIME: 45–50 MINUTES
SERVES 8

1½ cups all-purpose flour

1 teaspoon ground cinnamon

1 tablespoon baking powder

⅔ cup quinoa flakes

½ cup walnut halves, coarsely chopped

½ cup honey, plus extra, to serve

2 eggs

⅓ cup sunflower oil

¼ cup sour cream

2 cups (about 1 lb) mashed banana

Fresh ricotta cheese, to serve

1 Preheat the oven to 350°F. Lightly brush a 4 x 8 inch loaf pan with oil and line the base with parchment paper.

2 Sift the flour, cinnamon, baking powder and a pinch of salt into a large mixing bowl. Add the quinoa flakes and ⅓ cup of the walnuts and stir to combine.

3 Combine the honey, eggs, oil, sour cream and banana in a separate bowl. Add to the dry ingredients and stir until just combined.

4 Spoon the mixture into the prepared pan and smooth the surface with the back of the spoon. Sprinkle the remaining walnuts over the top. Bake for 45–50 minutes or until golden and a skewer inserted into the center comes out clean. Cover the top with foil if the loaf is browning too quickly.

5 Remove from the oven and set aside to cool for 10 minutes before turning out onto a wire rack. Serve warm or at room temperature with fresh ricotta and a drizzle of extra honey.

TIPS To make Banana & blueberry bread, omit the walnuts and stir through 1 cup fresh (or frozen) blueberries at the end of step 3.

This banana bread is great to freeze and can then be toasted straight from the freezer for a quick breakfast. Just cut into slices, wrap in plastic wrap and freeze for up to 2 months.

* Quinoa flakes are ideal to use in baked goods where you would typically use rolled oats.

Chickpea, tomato & quinoa soup with pesto toasts

PREPARATION TIME: 20 MINUTES
COOKING TIME: 35 MINUTES
SERVES 4

1½ tablespoons olive oil

1 large red onion, finely chopped

1 large celery rib, diced

2 cloves garlic, crushed

1 long red chile, seeded and finely chopped

1 teaspoon ground cumin

2 teaspoons sweet paprika

1½ tablespoons concentrated tomato purée

1 can (14 oz) chickpeas, drained and rinsed

⅓ cup quinoa (see tips), briefly rinsed

1 can (14 oz) chopped tomatoes

3 cups vegetable or chicken broth (see tips)

8 slices sourdough baguette or gluten-free bread

Good-quality basil pesto (see tips), to serve

1 Heat the oil in a large saucepan over medium heat and cook the onion and celery, stirring, for 5–6 minutes or until soft. Add the garlic, chile and spices and cook, stirring, for 1 minute, then add the tomato purée and cook, stirring, for 1 minute more.

2 Add the chickpeas, quinoa, tomatoes and broth and bring to the boil. Reduce the heat to low, partially cover and simmer for 25 minutes. Set aside to cool slightly.

3 Blend half the soup until smooth and return to the saucepan with the remaining soup. Place over medium heat, season with sea salt and freshly ground black pepper and warm through.

4 Meanwhile, toast the slices of bread until golden and then spread each with a little basil pesto. Serve the soup with the pesto toasts.

TIPS You can use either white or red quinoa in this recipe.
   If you want this soup to be gluten-free make sure you use gluten-free broth and pesto.
   This soup freezes well (without the pesto toasts). Simply place the cooled soup in airtight containers and freeze.

* *This soup is perfect for vegetarians, as combining legumes (chickpeas) with a whole grain such as quinoa makes this a complete protein and therefore a balanced meal.*

Spiced quinoa, sweet potato, broccoli & cranberry salad

PREPARATION TIME: 20 MINUTES
COOKING TIME: 25–30 MINUTES
SERVES 4

1½ lb sweet potatoes (about 2–3), peeled and cut into ¾ inch dice

¼ cup olive oil

1 cup quinoa (see tip), briefly rinsed

½ teaspoon ground turmeric

1 teaspoon ground cumin

½ lb broccoli, trimmed and cut into small florets (about 2 cups)

1 bunch asparagus (about 5 oz), trimmed and cut into ¾ inch lengths

⅓ cup dried cranberries

⅓ cup coarsely chopped mixed herbs (such as chives, parsley, mint)

3 tablespoons fresh orange juice

1½ tablespoons white balsamic vinegar

1 Preheat the oven to 400°F. Place the sweet potatoes on a large baking sheet lined with parchment paper. Drizzle with 1 tablespoon of the olive oil and season with sea salt and pepper. Roast for 25–30 minutes or until golden and tender.

2 Meanwhile, put the quinoa, turmeric, cumin and 2 cups water in a medium saucepan and bring to a boil. Reduce the heat to low, cover and simmer for 12 minutes or until the water is absorbed. Remove from the heat and set aside to cool slightly.

3 Blanch the broccoli and asparagus in a saucepan of boiling water until tender-crisp, then drain and refresh under cold running water.

4 Put the cooked quinoa, sweet potato, blanched vegetables, cranberries and herbs in a large bowl. Whisk together the remaining 3 tablespoons of olive oil, the orange juice and balsamic. Add to the salad and toss to combine, then season with sea salt and freshly ground black pepper, to taste.

TIP We used equal quantities of red and white quinoa in this recipe. There is no need to cook them separately.

* *The sweet potato and quinoa give this salad a low GI rating. If you have any leftovers, take them to work for a lunch that will provide slow-release energy throughout the day.*

PARMESAN & HERB
CHICKEN SCHNITZELS
WITH TOMATO SALSA
(PAGE 26)

Parmesan & herb chicken schnitzels with tomato salsa

PREPARATION TIME: 20 MINUTES

COOKING TIME: 15 MINUTES

SERVES 4

1 cup quinoa flakes

⅓ cup (1 oz) finely grated Parmesan cheese

3 tablespoons finely snipped chives

3 tablespoons finely chopped flat-leaf parsley

1 teaspoon finely grated lemon zest

¼ cup all-purpose flour (see tip)

2 eggs, lightly whisked

¼ cup milk

1½ lb chicken tenderloins or 4 x 6–7 oz chicken breasts (cut into 4 equal pieces)

3 tablespoons olive oil, approximately

Salad leaves, to serve

TOMATO SALSA

3 ripe plum tomatoes (about 4 oz each), diced

½ teaspoon dried red chile flakes

2 teaspoons red wine vinegar

2 tablespoons olive oil

1 Combine the quinoa flakes, Parmesan, herbs and lemon zest in a shallow bowl. Put the flour in a second shallow bowl and season with salt and pepper. Put the combined eggs and milk in a third bowl.

2 Dust a piece of chicken in the seasoned flour, then dip in the egg mixture and finally press into the quinoa mixture until it is evenly coated. Place on a tray and repeat to coat the remaining chicken.

3 To make the tomato salsa, put all the ingredients in a medium bowl and stir to combine. Season with a pinch of sugar, sea salt and freshly ground black pepper, to taste. Set aside.

4 Heat the oil in a large nonstick skillet over medium-high heat. Cook the crumbed chicken, in batches, for 3 minutes each side or until golden and cooked through, adding a little more oil to the skillet as necessary.

5 Serve the chicken schnitzels with the tomato salsa and salad leaves.

TIP If you would like these delicious schnitzels to be gluten free, simply replace the all-purpose flour with rice flour.

＊ *Quinoa flakes are fantastic for crumbing meat, chicken, fish, fishcakes or patties. They stick easily, become crisp and golden once pan-fried, and have more flavor than bread crumbs.*

Red lentil & quinoa dhal

PREPARATION TIME: 20 MINUTES
COOKING TIME: 35–40 MINUTES
SERVES 4

1½ tablespoons sunflower oil

1 medium red onion, finely chopped

2 teaspoons finely grated ginger

1 long red chile, seeded and
finely chopped

2 cloves garlic, crushed

1 teaspoon ground coriander

2 teaspoons ground cumin

12 fresh curry leaves (see tips),
plus extra, to garnish

½ cup split red lentils, briefly rinsed

½ cup quinoa (see tips),
briefly rinsed

1½ tablespoons lime juice

Sugar, to taste

Plain yogurt, to garnish

Poppadoms (see tips), to serve

1 Heat the oil in a large saucepan over medium heat. Add the onion and cook, stirring occasionally, for 5 minutes or until soft. Add the ginger, chile, garlic, spices and curry leaves and cook for 1–2 minutes or until fragrant.

2 Add the lentils, quinoa and 3 cups water and bring to a boil. Reduce the heat to low and simmer, stirring occasionally, for 25–30 minutes or until the lentils and quinoa are soft but still have some texture, and the mixture is thick. Stir through the lime juice and season with sugar, sea salt and freshly ground black pepper, to taste.

3 Garnish with the yogurt and extra curry leaves, and serve with the poppadoms.

TIPS Fresh curry leaves can be found at South Asian supermarkets.
   We used red quinoa in this recipe.
   If you do not require this meal to be gluten free, you can serve it with naan bread instead of the poppadoms.
   If you like your dhal really spicy, try adding ½ teaspoon dried red chile flakes with the spices in step 1.
   This dhal makes a fantastic dip to serve at parties, and can be eaten warm or at room temperature.

* *Adding quinoa to dhal makes this dish ideal for vegetarians or vegans, as lentils and quinoa are complementary proteins.*

Pancetta, spinach & leek frittata

PREPARATION TIME: 20 MINUTES
COOKING TIME: 50–55 MINUTES
SERVES 6

½ cup quinoa (see tips), briefly rinsed

1½ tablespoons olive oil

3–4 oz pancetta (see tips), diced

1 large leek, white part only,
thinly sliced

1 clove garlic, crushed

4½ cups (7 oz) baby spinach leaves

8 eggs

¾ cup milk

⅓ cup (1 oz) finely grated
Parmesan cheese

3 oz goat's cheese, crumbled

1½ tablespoons snipped chives

Arugula leaves, to serve

* *Quinoa is a great source of slow-release carbohydrates. Just add some salad leaves to make this frittata a balanced meal, containing carbohydrates, protein and vegetables.*

1 Preheat the oven to 350°F. Lightly grease an 8 x 12 inch rectangular baking dish and line the base with parchment paper. Put the quinoa in a small saucepan with 1 cup water and bring to a boil. Reduce the heat to low, cover and simmer for 12 minutes or until the water is absorbed. Remove from the heat and set aside to cool slightly.

2 Heat the oil in a medium skillet over medium heat. Cook the pancetta and leek, stirring occasionally, for 5 minutes or until golden. Add the garlic and cook, stirring, for 1 minute. Remove from the heat and set aside.

3 Put the spinach in a large heatproof bowl and pour over enough boiling water to cover. Blanch for 30 seconds, then drain and refresh under cold running water. Drain well, squeezing out any excess water. Coarsely chop.

4 Whisk the eggs and milk together in a large bowl. Stir through the quinoa, leek mixture, spinach and Parmesan. Pour into the prepared dish, dot the goat's cheese over the top and sprinkle with the chives. Bake for 30–35 minutes or until the frittata is set, puffed and golden.

5 Serve the frittata warm or cold, cut into squares and accompanied by arugula leaves.

TIPS We used white quinoa in this recipe.
   Some pancetta may contain gluten, so always check the label.
   This frittata is ideal for lunch boxes and picnic baskets.
   To make a richer and creamier version of this frittata, replace the milk with light cream (18% MF).

Quinoa, feta, roasted bell pepper & corn muffins

PREPARATION TIME: 20 MINUTES
COOKING TIME: 20 MINUTES
MAKES 12

1½ cups self-rising flour (see tips)

1 cup quinoa flakes

1 cup corn kernels (fresh, canned or frozen)

²/3 cup (4 oz) drained roasted bell pepper in oil, diced

3 oz feta cheese, crumbled

3 tablespoons snipped chives

1 cup milk

1 egg

1/3 cup sunflower oil

1 Preheat the oven to 350°F. Line a 12-cup muffin tin with paper liners.

2 Sift the flour into a large bowl and stir through the quinoa flakes, corn, bell pepper, feta and chives. Combine the milk, egg and oil in a large jug, add to the dry ingredients and stir until well combined (do not overmix).

3 Divide the mixture among the lined muffin cups and bake for 20 minutes or until golden and cooked through. Set aside for 5 minutes to cool, then transfer to a wire rack. Serve warm or at room temperature.

TIPS If you do not have self-rising flour, substitute 1½ cups all-purpose flour, 1½ teaspoons baking powder and ½ teaspoon salt.

These muffins can be frozen for up to 1 month, wrapped well in plastic wrap. Thaw at room temperature.

* I love adding quinoa flakes to baked goods such as these muffins. They taste great and also add protein, calcium, iron and B vitamins, making them the perfect addition to lunch boxes.

Vegetables stuffed with quinoa, lamb, pine nuts & currants

PREPARATION TIME: 20 MINUTES
COOKING TIME: 50–55 MINUTES
SERVES 4

½ cup quinoa, briefly rinsed

4 large (about 5 oz each) vine-ripened tomatoes

4 zucchini (about 7 oz each)

½ lb ground lamb

1 teaspoon ground allspice

4 scallions, trimmed and thinly sliced

3 tablespoons dried currants

3 tablespoons coarsely chopped mint

3 tablespoons coarsely chopped flat-leaf parsley

¼ cup pine nuts, lightly toasted

3 oz creamy feta cheese, crumbled

Salad leaves, to serve

1 Preheat the oven to 350°F. Line a large baking sheet with parchment paper. Put the quinoa in a small saucepan with 1 cup water and bring to a boil. Reduce the heat to low, cover and simmer for 12 minutes or until the water is absorbed. Remove from the heat and set aside to cool completely.

2 Meanwhile, cut off the top of each tomato. Scoop out the flesh and pulp and reserve, leaving a ½ inch thick shell. Cut each zucchini in half lengthways. Scoop out the flesh and discard, leaving a ½ inch thick shell.

3 Coarsely chop the reserved tomato flesh and put in a large bowl with the reserved tomato pulp, cooked quinoa, ground lamb, allspice, scallions, currants, herbs, pine nuts and feta. Stir until all the ingredients are well combined, then season with sea salt and freshly ground black pepper.

4 Stuff each tomato and zucchini shell with the quinoa mixture. Place the stuffed zucchini on the lined baking sheet and bake for 15 minutes. Add the stuffed tomatoes to the baking sheet and bake for a further 20–25 minutes or until the zucchini and tomatoes are tender and the stuffing is golden. Serve with salad leaves.

TIPS We used white quinoa in this recipe.
For a vegetarian version, omit the lamb, increase the quinoa to 1 cup and increase the water to 2 cups.

* *Stuffed vegetables traditionally contain bread crumbs, couscous or cracked wheat. Quinoa is a great gluten-free alternative and it works beautifully with the Middle Eastern flavors in this recipe.*

Chunky chocolate, quinoa & pecan cookies

PREPARATION TIME: 15 MINUTES

COOKING TIME: 12–15 MINUTES

MAKES ABOUT 18

½ cup plus 1 tablespoon unsalted butter, softened

2/3 cup lightly packed light brown sugar

1 egg, lightly whisked

1 teaspoon natural vanilla extract

3/4 cup all-purpose flour

1 teaspoon baking powder

1 cup quinoa flakes

1 cup chopped milk chocolate, or chocolate chips

2/3 cup pecan nuts, chopped

* *The combination of chocolate, pecans and brown sugar with the nutty taste of quinoa flakes makes these cookies absolutely delicious.*

1 Preheat the oven to 350°F and line 2 baking sheets with parchment paper.

2 Use an electric mixer to cream the butter and sugar until pale and creamy. Add the egg and vanilla and beat until well combined. Sift the flour and baking powder together, add to the butter mixture and stir until combined. Add the quinoa flakes, chocolate and pecan nuts and stir until just combined.

3 Roll rounded tablespoons of the mixture into balls and place on the lined baking sheets, 1½ inches apart. Flatten the balls with a fork dipped in flour, then bake for 12–15 minutes or until pale golden.

4 Remove from the oven and cool on the baking sheets for 5 minutes before transferring to a wire rack to cool completely.

TIPS For a gluten-free version, replace the all-purpose flour with 1/3 cup rice flour, and 2 oz gluten-free all-purpose flour.

For a nut-free version, replace the pecans with chopped dates or dried cranberries.

Store these cookies in an airtight container for up to 5 days.

Carrot quinoa cake with cream cheese frosting

PREPARATION TIME: 20 MINUTES
(+ COOLING)
COOKING TIME: 50 MINUTES
SERVES 12

1½ cups gluten-free self-rising flour (see tips)

1 teaspoon ground cinnamon

½ teaspoon ground nutmeg

1 cup lightly packed light brown sugar

½ cup ground almonds

1 cup cooked quinoa (see page 15)

1½ cups (8 oz) firmly packed shredded carrot

½ cup seedless raisins, coarsely chopped

¾ cup vegetable oil

3 eggs

FROSTING

8 oz cream cheese, softened

1 teaspoon finely grated orange zest

⅓ cup pure confectioners' or icing sugar, sifted

3 tablespoons freshly squeezed orange juice, strained

* *The cooked quinoa gives this cake a delicious moist texture.*

1 Preheat the oven to 350°F. Grease a square 8 inch cake pan and line with parchment paper.

2 Sift the flour, cinnamon and nutmeg together into a large mixing bowl. Add the sugar, ground almonds, quinoa, carrot and raisins and stir to combine. Whisk the oil and eggs together, add to the quinoa mixture and stir until well combined.

3 Spoon the batter into the prepared pan and bake for 50 minutes or until the cake is firm to touch and a skewer inserted into the center comes out with only a few moist crumbs clinging to it. (You may need to cover the cake with foil if it is browning too quickly.) Transfer the pan to a wire rack and set aside to cool for 15 minutes. Remove the cake from the pan and set aside on the wire rack to cool completely.

4 To make the frosting, use an electric mixer to beat the cream cheese and orange zest until smooth. Add the confectioners' sugar and orange juice and beat until well combined. Spread evenly over the top and sides of the cooled carrot cake and serve.

TIP If you don't require this cake to be gluten free, use 1½ cups wheat self-rising flour instead of the gluten-free flour.

To create your own self-rising flour combine 1½ cups all-purpose flour, 1½ teaspoons baking powder and ½ teaspoon salt.

This cake will keep, stored in an airtight container in a cool place, for up to 3 days.

Amaranth

NUTRITIONAL INFORMATION
(per 9 oz/1 cup cooked amaranth)

Energy: 1051 kilojoules, 251 calories   Protein: 9.3 g   Total fat: 3.9 g

Saturated fat: 0 g   Carbohydrate: 46 g   Sugars: 0 g   Dietary fiber: 5.2 g

Cholesterol: 0 mg   Vitamin B_6: 0.3 mg   Iron: 5.2 mg   Magnesium: 160 mg

Manganese: 2.1 mg   Phosphorus: 364 mg   Sodium: 14.8 mg

Gluten free

Amaranth

Amaranth is a pseudo-grain, like quinoa, grown by the ancient Aztecs over 5000 years ago. Its name is derived from the Greek *amarantos,* which means 'unfading'. Amaranth was a staple crop not only to the Aztecs, but also the Incas and Mayans, until its cultivation was banned by the invading Spanish conquistadors as it was often used in local religious rituals.

Amaranth plants are a member of the goosefoot family, and therefore related to spinach. They produce tiny edible seeds, with up to 500,000 per plant, and their leaves are also highly nutritious and edible.

When amaranth experienced a revival in the 1970s, wild varieties found in Mexico were grown for commercial use. Today, amaranth is again growing in popularity. The recent attention it is receiving is mainly due to its impressive nutritional qualities. It is gluten and wheat free, so it is suitable for those with celiac disease or wheat intolerances. It is also a good source of vegetable protein (13–14%) due to its amino acid balance, particularly the presence of lysine, an amino acid that is missing or negligible in most other grains.

Amaranth grain has a glycemic index of just 21, so it is considered a low-GI food. This makes it ideal for diabetics or those following a low-GI diet. It is also rich in phytosterols, which are linked to reducing cholesterol.

Amaranth is packed with vitamins and minerals, in particular calcium, iron, magnesium, manganese, phosphorus, vitamin E, and B vitamins. Amaranth also contains good fats, with an oil content of 6–9% which is higher than most other grains. Amaranth oil is high in unsaturated fatty acids, especially linoleic acid.

Amaranth is available as a whole grain, puffed and as flour. Amaranth grains are tiny, similar in size and color to brown mustard seeds. Like quinoa it has a central seed and an outer germ that uncurls during cooking.

Amaranth grain cooks relatively quickly, in about 20 minutes; however, it is a little trickier and less forgiving than quinoa, which explains why it has not gained as much popularity. Once cooked, it releases a starch and develops a slightly sticky texture on standing, so it's best combined with another grain, such as brown rice, millet or quinoa, if you want to use it in salads. As a general rule, I'd suggest using one part amaranth to three parts another grain. The natural stickiness of amaranth does work in its favour when making porridge, however.

Amaranth flour can be used in gluten-free baked goods that do not require leavening such as flat breads, brownies and cookies. It can also be substituted for approximately one-quarter of the flour in leavened baked products such as bread. It has quite a distinct herbaceous flavor that can be a little overpowering on its own.

Puffed amaranth is my favorite form of amaranth, and it has the mildest flavor of the three. It gives a delicious crisp texture when added to granola and breakfast cereals, cookies, granola bars and other baked goods. You can make puffed amaranth yourself, but it tends to burn easily, so it is much easier to buy it already made. A common treat made in Mexico is alegria, made from puffed amaranth, honey and chocolate.

To cook amaranth

Toasting amaranth grain before cooking tends to soften the flavor slightly and is generally preferred. Place 1 cup amaranth in a skillet over medium heat. Cook, stirring, for 3 minutes or until just fragrant. Transfer to a saucepan, add 2½ cups water and bring to the boil. Reduce the heat to low, cover and simmer for 20 minutes or until the grain is *al dente* and the mixture has thickened.

Andean grain salad with salmon, red grapes & watercress

PREPARATION TIME: 20 MINUTES
(+ COOLING)
COOKING TIME: 20 MINUTES
SERVES 4

1 cup Andean grain mix (see tips), briefly rinsed

2 x 6–7 oz skinless salmon fillets

3 tablespoons olive oil, plus 2 teaspoons, extra

8 oz (2½ cups) sugar snap peas, trimmed

7 oz (1½ cups) seedless red grapes, halved

2 cups picked watercress sprigs (about 2 oz, see tips), washed

4 oz creamy feta cheese, crumbled

¼ cup snipped chives

2 tablespoons lemon juice

1 teaspoon finely grated lemon zest

½ teaspoon sugar

1 Put the grain mix in a medium saucepan with 2 cups water and bring to a boil. Reduce the heat to low, cover and simmer for 12 minutes or until the water is absorbed. Remove from the heat and set aside to cool completely.

2 Brush the salmon fillets with the extra olive oil. Heat a medium nonstick skillet over high heat and cook the salmon for 2–3 minutes each side (for medium) or until cooked to your liking. Remove and set aside to cool slightly, then break up the salmon into large flakes.

3 Blanch the sugar snaps in a saucepan of boiling water until they are tender-crisp. Drain and refresh under cold running water.

4 Put the cooked grain mix, salmon, sugar snaps, grapes, watercress, feta and chives in a large bowl. Whisk the olive oil, lemon juice, zest and sugar together. Add to the salad and gently toss to combine, then season with sea salt and freshly ground black pepper to taste.

TIPS Andean grain mix is also sometimes called 'supergrain mix' and is a combination of amaranth and red, white and black quinoa. To make your own, simply combine equal quantities of these grains.

You can replace the watercress leaves with baby arugula or spinach leaves if you like.

> ✳ *Amaranth grain is rich in the minerals manganese, iron, magnesium and phosphorus. It is also packed with dietary fiber and is a great vegetable source of protein. It becomes slightly sticky when cooked so it is best combined with quinoa when used as a salad grain.*

Amaranth & raisin cookies

PREPARATION TIME: 15 MINUTES
COOKING TIME: 15 MINUTES
MAKES ABOUT 24

6 tablespoons unsalted butter

3 tablespoons crunchy peanut butter

3 tablespoons honey

1 cup all-purpose flour (see tips)

½ teaspoon ground ginger

2 cups puffed amaranth

⅓ cup sugar

⅓ cup firmly packed light brown sugar

½ cup raisins

1 egg, lightly whisked

1 Preheat the oven to 350°F and line 2 large baking sheets with parchment paper. Put the butter, peanut butter and honey in a small saucepan over medium heat and stir occasionally until the butter has melted. Set aside to cool slightly.

2 Sift the flour and ginger into a large mixing bowl. Add the amaranth, sugars, raisins, cooled butter mixture and egg and stir until well combined.

3 Using slightly wet hands, roll rounded tablespoons of the mixture into balls and place on the lined baking sheets, 1½ inches apart. You need to roll each ball in your hand until it becomes sticky, about 30 seconds. Use a lightly floured fork to flatten the balls slightly, then bake for 10–12 minutes or until golden.

4 Remove from the oven and cool on the baking sheets for 5 minutes before transferring to a wire rack to cool completely.

TIPS If you would like to make these cookies gluten-free, substitute the all-purpose flour with amaranth flour, or use ½ cup rice flour and ½ cup gluten-free all-purpose flour.
    These cookies will keep in an airtight container for up to 5 days.

* Puffed amaranth adds a delicious crisp texture to baked goods such as cookies and granola bars.

AMARANTH & MILLET
PORRIDGE WITH PISTACHIO
SEED SPRINKLE (PAGE 46)

Amaranth & millet porridge with pistachio seed sprinkle

PREPARATION TIME: 10 MINUTES
COOKING TIME: 30–35 MINUTES
SERVES 4

¾ cup hulled millet

¼ cup amaranth

½ teaspoon ground cinnamon

1 cup milk

⅓ cup dried apricots, chopped

**Greek-style yogurt and honey,
to serve**

PISTACHIO SEED SPRINKLE
⅓ cup pistachios, chopped
¼ cup pumpkin seeds
¼ cup sunflower seeds
3 tablespoons sesame seeds
1½ tablespoons light brown sugar

1 Preheat the oven to 350°F and line a baking sheet with parchment paper. To make the pistachio seed sprinkle, put all the ingredients in a bowl and stir to combine. Spread the mixture over the lined baking sheet and bake for 5–10 minutes or until golden. Set aside to cool.

2 Meanwhile, put the millet, amaranth and cinnamon in a large saucepan with $2\frac{1}{2}$ cups water and bring to a boil. Reduce the heat to low, cover and simmer, stirring occasionally, for 20 minutes or until the water is absorbed. Add the milk and apricots, cover and simmer, stirring occasionally, for 5–10 minutes or until the porridge is thick and creamy and the grains are tender.

3 Serve the porridge topped with a spoonful of yogurt, a drizzle of honey and some pistachio seed sprinkle.

TIP The pistachio seed sprinkle will keep in an airtight container for up to 2 weeks. It is also delicious sprinkled over fruit and yogurt.

> * *Amaranth is well suited for making porridge because it becomes slightly sticky when cooked with liquid. Amaranth and millet have similar cooking times so are an ideal combination for a gluten-free breakfast.*

Amaranth, cashew & apricot balls

PREPARATION TIME: 15 MINUTES
COOKING TIME: 2 MINUTES
MAKES ABOUT 20

1 cup rolled oats

⅓ cup dried cranberries

⅓ cup chopped dried apricots

¼ cup chopped semisweet chocolate,
or chocolate chips

1 cup puffed amaranth

¼ cup cashew spread

⅓ cup honey

½ cup shredded coconut

1 Line a large baking sheet with parchment paper. Put the oats, cranberries, apricots and chocolate in a food processor and process until they are finely chopped. Transfer to a large bowl and mix in the puffed amaranth.

2 Put the cashew spread and honey in a small saucepan over low heat. Warm gently and stir until combined. Add the honey mixture to the dry ingredients and mix until well combined.

3 Place the coconut on a plate. Using slightly wet hands (to prevent sticking) roll tablespoons of the mixture into balls, then press in the coconut to lightly coat. Cover and refrigerate until firm.

TIPS These are perfect for after-school snacks or lunch boxes.
For a nut-free version, replace the cashew spread with tahini or nut-free butter.

* Puffed amaranth can be used in recipes where you would typically use plain puffed rice cereal, such as granola bars, cookies and slices. Amaranth is rich in protein and dietary fiber, and is easily digested as it is gluten free. Here it's combined with rolled oats, nuts and dried fruit, making little snacks that are packed with nutrients.

Gluten-free granola with dried apple, pumpkin seeds & almonds

PREPARATION TIME: 15 MINUTES
COOKING TIME: NIL
MAKES ABOUT 6½ CUPS

1½ cups puffed amaranth
1½ cups puffed millet
1 cup rice bran flakes
½ cup roasted buckwheat groats
2/3 cup chopped dried apple
¾ cup dried cranberries
¾ cup almonds, coarsely chopped
½ cup pumpkin seeds
3 tablespoons flaxseeds
¼ cup sunflower seeds

1 Put all the ingredients in a large bowl and mix to combine. Transfer to an airtight container and store until needed.

TIPS For a wheat-free version, add some rolled oats.

This granola will keep for about 2 weeks in an airtight container in a cool dark place.

* *This gluten-free granola runs rings around the commercial varieties, which can often be bland. The puffed amaranth and millet add lots of flavor, while the roasted buckwheat gives body, texture and a nutty taste.*

This granola is packed with protein, complex carbohydrates and dietary fiber, plus the nuts and seeds provide good oils, just what you need to start your day.

Little passion fruit & coconut cakes

PREPARATION TIME: 15 MINUTES
COOKING TIME: 20 MINUTES
MAKES 12

2¼ cups pure confectioners' or icing sugar, sifted, plus extra, to serve

½ cup amaranth flour

½ teaspoon baking powder (see tips)

1 cup ground almonds

½ cup shredded coconut

6 egg whites, lightly whisked

½ cup unsalted butter, melted and cooled

1 teaspoon finely grated lime zest

¼ cup passion fruit pulp (see tips)

1 Preheat the oven to 350°F. Line a 12-cup muffin tin with paper liners.

2 Sift the confectioners' sugar, amaranth flour and baking powder together into a large bowl. Stir in the ground almonds and coconut.

3 Add the egg whites, butter, lime zest and passion fruit pulp and stir to combine. Divide the mixture among the lined muffin cups.

4 Bake for 20 minutes or until golden and cooked through (a skewer inserted into the center of a cake should come out with a few moist crumbs clinging to it). Remove from the oven and set aside for 5 minutes, then transfer to a wire rack to cool. Serve dusted with extra confectioners' sugar.

TIPS If you want these cakes to be gluten free, make sure you use gluten-free baking powder.

You will need about 3 passion fruit to get this amount of pulp.

The cakes will keep, in an airtight container, for up to 3 days.

> * *Amaranth flour has quite a herbaceous flavor, so it works well with the nuttiness of almond meal. Amaranth flour is gluten free, so it is ideal to use in gluten-free baking.*

Buckwheat

NUTRITIONAL INFORMATION
(per 6 oz/1 cup cooked buckwheat)

Energy: 649 kilojoules, 155 calories Protein: 5.7 g Total fat: 1 g

Saturated fat: 0.2 g Carbohydrate: 33.5 g Sugars: 1.5 g Dietary fiber: 4.5 g

Cholesterol: 0 mg Iron: 1.3 mg Magnesium: 85.7 mg Manganese: 0.7 mg

Phosphorus: 118 mg Sodium: 6.7 mg

Gluten free

Buckwheat

Buckwheat is not a type of wheat, but is the triangular seed of a plant related to rhubarb and sorrel. Although technically a pseudo-grain, it is widely classified and utilized as a grain, and is a great substitute for those sensitive to wheat or gluten. Buckwheat is also quick to prepare, a high-quality vegetable protein and rich in various nutrients and phytochemicals, making it a wonderful addition to any diet.

Buckwheat is an ancient crop, first cultivated in South-East Asia around 6000 BC, from where it spread to Central Asia, Europe and the Middle East. It grows better in cooler climates and is a short-season crop. In the mountainous regions of northern China and Tibet, where wheat cannot be grown, buckwheat has long been used to make buckwheat noodles. Today, the top producers of buckwheat are Russia and China. One of the best known uses of buckwheat would have to be in the small buckwheat pancakes, called blini, originally from Russia. Buckwheat porridge made from the grains (also known as groats) is a peasant dish in eastern Europe.

While buckwheat (soba) noodles and pancakes may be familiar to many, buckwheat grain tends to be underutilized in Western countries. This is mainly due to a lack of knowledge on how to use and prepare it properly. However, a growing awareness of its unique nutritional qualities is gradually increasing its popularity, especially with those following a wheat-free, gluten-free or vegetarian diet.

Buckwheat is a quality source of a complete vegetable protein (13–15%), containing all essential amino acids, so it is an ideal food for vegetarians and vegans. It is an excellent source of manganese and magnesium, and a good source of niacin, folate, iron, zinc, copper, selenium and phosphorus.

Buckwheat is also rich in phytochemicals. Of particular interest is the antioxidant rutin, which is believed to help lower cholesterol and reduce blood pressure. It is a great source of polyunsaturated fatty acids, such as linoleic acid, as well as being high in soluble fiber, aiding gastrointestinal health.

Buckwheat can be purchased in its hulled grain form (known as groats), as a flour or as puffed buckwheat. It can also be purchased in its processed form, as pasta or noodles. It has a distinct earthy flavor that can polarize people, but it definitely grows on you the more you eat it.

Buckwheat kernels are triangular in shape and have a hard inedible hull that must be removed. The groats can be purchased either raw or toasted. Toasted buckwheat can have quite a strong flavor that often disguises stale buckwheat. I find buying the raw version and toasting it myself gives a milder and far superior result. Buckwheat kernels can be used in salads, in porridge or as an alternative to rice in risotto and pilafs.

Buckwheat flour is made from grinding the kernels and has a strong earthy flavor. It is used to make noodles, pancakes and bread, and is often combined with some wheat flour to tone down the taste. Puffed buckwheat is a delicious addition to home-made granola, or baked goods such as granola bars.

To cook buckwheat

To toast buckwheat, heat a large nonstick skillet over medium-high heat. Add 1 cup raw buckwheat kernels and cook, stirring, for 3–4 minutes or until just fragrant.

To cook, put the toasted buckwheat and 2 cups water in a saucepan and bring to a boil. Cover, reduce the heat to low and simmer for 10–12 minutes or until just tender (be careful not to overcook). Rinse under cold running water; drain well.

Roasted beet, buckwheat & goat's cheese salad

PREPARATION TIME: 20 MINUTES
(+ COOLING)
COOKING TIME: 45 MINUTES
SERVES 4

10–12 (about 1–1½ lb in total) baby beets, trimmed

1 cup raw buckwheat groats

½ cup hazelnuts, lightly toasted and skinned

4 oz (about 3 cups) baby arugula leaves

3 tablespoons snipped chives

4 oz soft goat's cheese (see tips), crumbled

DRESSING

3 tablespoons olive oil

3 tablespoons fresh orange juice

1½ tablespoons balsamic vinegar

1 Preheat the oven to 400°F. Put the beets in a large roasting pan, cover the pan with foil and roast for 40–45 minutes or until they are tender when pierced with a skewer. Set aside to cool slightly, then peel (see tips) and cut into wedges.

2 Meanwhile, heat a large nonstick skillet over medium-high heat. Add the buckwheat and cook, stirring, for 3–4 minutes or until fragrant. Put the toasted buckwheat and 2 cups water in a saucepan and bring to a boil. Cover, reduce the heat to low and simmer for 10–12 minutes or until just tender (be careful not to overcook). Rinse under cold running water, then drain well.

3 Coarsely chop the hazelnuts and place in a large bowl. Add the beets, cooked buckwheat, arugula and chives and stir to combine.

4 To make the dressing, whisk the olive oil, orange juice and balsamic in a small bowl until combined. Add to the salad and toss well. Sprinkle with the goat's cheese and season with sea salt and freshly ground black pepper, to taste.

TIPS Wear gloves while peeling the beets to prevent your hands becoming stained by the juices.

You could substitute a creamy feta cheese or marinated feta for the goat's cheese if you like.

⁎ The earthy flavor of the buckwheat is delicious with roasted beets and goat's cheese. Buckwheat is an ideal grain for vegetarian dishes such as this, as it is rich in protein, B vitamins, calcium and phosphorus. The cheese and hazelnuts also add extra protein.

Soba noodles with beef & miso broth

PREPARATION TIME: 20 MINUTES
COOKING TIME: 25 MINUTES
SERVES 4

3 cups beef broth

2 teaspoons finely grated ginger

3 tablespoons soy sauce

1½ tablespoons mirin (Japanese cooking wine)

6 oz dried soba noodles

1½ tablespoons sunflower oil

1 large white onion, thinly sliced

3 tablespoons white or yellow (brown) miso paste

1 bunch (about 13 oz) baby bok choy, trimmed

10 oz beef tenderloin, thinly sliced (see tip)

Thinly sliced scallion, to garnish

1 Put the broth, 3 cups water, the ginger, soy sauce and mirin in a large saucepan and bring to a boil. Reduce the heat to low and simmer for 5 minutes. Remove from the heat and set aside.

2 Cook the noodles in a large saucepan of salted boiling water, following the packet instructions, until *al dente*. Drain well, then divide among four serving bowls.

3 Clean the saucepan and return to medium heat. Add the oil and cook the onion, stirring, for 5 minutes or until softened. Add the broth mixture and bring to a simmer, then whisk in the miso paste until smooth. Add the bok choy and simmer for 1 minute, then remove from the heat. Add the beef and stir to combine (the heat of the soup will cook the beef).

4 Ladle the hot soup over the noodles and serve garnished with the scallion.

TIP Partially freezing the beef makes it easier to slice it paper-thin.

* *Soba noodles are a great way to incorporate buckwheat into your diet. Most soba noodles contain wheat and buckwheat flour, so are not suitable for a gluten-free diet. You can buy gluten-free soba noodles made from 100% buckwheat from health food stores, but they are much stronger in flavor and do tend to stick a little, so make sure you rinse them well once cooked.*

Buckwheat pasta with pancetta, broccoli & chile

PREPARATION TIME: 20 MINUTES
COOKING TIME: 20 MINUTES
SERVES 4

1–1½ lb broccoli, trimmed and cut into florets (about 4–5 cups)

¼ cup (1 oz) finely grated Parmesan cheese, plus extra, to serve

10 oz buckwheat pasta (we used spirals)

1½ tablespoons olive oil

4 oz pancetta (see tips), diced

2 cloves garlic, crushed

1 teaspoon finely grated lemon zest

½ teaspoon dried red chile flakes

⅓ cup light cream (18% MF)

* *Buckwheat pasta is gluten free, so it is a great alternative to wheat pasta for those on a wheat-free or gluten-free diet. It is available from health food stores and some supermarkets. It has quite an earthy, nutty taste that is delicious with this simple broccoli sauce. Buckwheat pasta tends to cook a little faster than regular pasta — be careful not to overcook it as it doesn't hold its shape as well as wheat pasta.*

1 Cook the broccoli in a large saucepan of boiling water until bright green and tender-crisp. Drain, reserving ⅓ cup of the cooking liquid. Refresh the broccoli under cold running water, then drain well.

2 Put half the broccoli in a food processor (reserve the remaining broccoli) and add 3 tablespoons of the reserved cooking liquid and the Parmesan. Process until smooth, adding a little more of the cooking liquid if necessary.

3 Cook the pasta in salted boiling water according to the packet instructions, until *al dente*, then drain well.

4 Meanwhile, heat the oil in a large nonstick skillet and cook the pancetta, stirring occasionally, for 3–4 minutes or until golden. Add the garlic, zest and chile and cook, stirring, for 1 minute more. Stir in the reserved broccoli florets, the processed broccoli mixture and the cream and simmer for 2 minutes.

5 Add the pasta and toss together for 1–2 minutes or until the pasta is coated in the sauce and heated through. Season with sea salt and freshly ground black pepper and serve garnished with extra Parmesan.

TIPS Some pancetta may contain gluten, so always check the label.
    You can use spelt, kamut or wholemeal (whole-wheat) pasta instead of buckwheat pasta, but the dish will not be gluten free.

BUCKWHEAT & BROILED
CHICKEN SUMMER SALAD
(PAGE 64)

Buckwheat & broiled chicken summer salad

PREPARATION TIME: 20 MINUTES
(+ 30 MINUTES MARINATING)
COOKING TIME: 25 MINUTES
SERVES 4

¼ cup lemon juice

¼ cup olive oil

2 cloves garlic, crushed

1 lb skinless boneless chicken thighs, fat trimmed

1 cup raw buckwheat groats

1 small cucumber, trimmed and diced

2 cups (½ lb) mixed cherry and grape tomatoes, halved or quartered depending on size

¼ cup flat-leaf parsley leaves

¼ cup mint leaves, torn

¼ cup basil leaves, torn

4 scallions, trimmed and thinly sliced

1 teaspoon sumac (see tips), plus extra, to garnish

1 Put half the lemon juice, half the oil and the garlic in a shallow glass or ceramic container and stir to combine. Add the chicken and stir to coat. Cover and set aside for 30 minutes to marinate.

2 Meanwhile, heat a large nonstick skillet over medium-high heat. Add the buckwheat and cook, stirring, for 3–4 minutes or until fragrant. Put the toasted buckwheat and 2 cups water in a saucepan and bring to a boil. Cover, reduce the heat to low and simmer for 10–12 minutes or until just tender (be careful not to overcook). Rinse under cold running water, then drain well.

3 Transfer the buckwheat to a large mixing bowl and add the cucumber, tomatoes, herbs, scallions, sumac and the remaining lemon juice and olive oil. Stir to combine, then season with sea salt and freshly ground black pepper.

4 Preheat a chargrill pan over medium-high heat. Cook the chicken for 4 minutes each side or until lightly charred and cooked through. Set aside to cool slightly, then thinly slice. Add the chicken to the salad and toss to combine. Serve sprinkled with a little extra sumac.

TIPS Sumac is a spice used in Middle Eastern and Mediterranean cooking. It has a tangy citrus flavor and a vibrant deep-red color.
Toasting the buckwheat before cooking only takes a few minutes, but it results in a much better flavor so it is worth the effort. I find toasting it myself is better than buying commercial toasted buckwheat (known as kasha), as it can be very dark in color and overpowering in taste.

* *This flavorsome salad is similar to a tabouleh, but unlike the traditional cracked wheat version it is gluten free.*

Buckwheat risotto with lemon & garlic shrimp

PREPARATION TIME: 20 MINUTES

COOKING TIME: 40 MINUTES

SERVES 4

1½ tablespoons lemon juice

2 cloves garlic, crushed

2 teaspoons finely grated lemon zest

3 tablespoons olive oil

12 raw large shrimp, peeled and deveined with tails left intact

4 cups chicken broth (see tip)

1½ cups raw buckwheat groats

1½ tablespoons unsalted butter

1 large white onion, finely chopped

1 medium fennel bulb, trimmed and finely chopped

½ cup white wine

3 tablespoons light cream (18% MF)

⅓ cup (1 oz) finely grated Parmesan cheese

2¼ cups (4 oz) baby spinach leaves

* *When cooked in a risotto style, buckwheat is surprisingly creamy and has a delicious nutty flavor. It takes about the same time to cook as arborio rice, but has over three times as much dietary fiber.*

1 Put the lemon juice, half the garlic, half the lemon zest and half the olive oil in a shallow glass or ceramic bowl. Add the shrimp and stir until they are coated in the garlic mixture. Cover and set aside to marinate while you make the risotto.

2 Bring the chicken broth to a boil in a medium saucepan over high heat. Reduce the heat to very low and keep at a gentle simmer. Meanwhile, heat a large nonstick skillet over medium-high heat and cook the buckwheat, stirring, for 3–4 minutes or until fragrant. Remove from the heat and set aside.

3 Heat the butter and remaining olive oil in a large heavy-based saucepan over medium heat. Cook the onion and fennel, stirring, for 6–7 minutes or until softened. Add the remaining garlic and cook for 1 minute more. Add the toasted buckwheat and stir until the grains are well coated in the butter mixture.

4 Add the wine and simmer until it has almost evaporated. Start adding the broth, a ladleful at a time. Cook, stirring, until almost all the broth has evaporated before adding another ladleful.

5 When you have added all the broth and the buckwheat is *al dente* and creamy (this will take about 25 minutes), add the remaining lemon zest, the cream and Parmesan. Season with salt and pepper and stir to combine, then remove from the heat. Cover and stand for 5 minutes, then stir through the spinach leaves.

6 Meanwhile, heat a large nonstick skillet over high heat. Cook the shrimp for 1–2 minutes each side or until they are golden and just cooked through. To serve, divide the risotto among serving bowls and top each with 3 shrimp.

TIP If you want this dish to be gluten free, make sure you use gluten-free broth.

Buckwheat, corn & chive fritters with crisp bacon

PREPARATION TIME: 20 MINUTES
COOKING TIME: 20 MINUTES
SERVES 4

¾ cup milk

2 eggs, separated

½ cup all-purpose flour

½ cup buckwheat flour

2 teaspoons baking powder

2 cups fresh corn kernels

1 zucchini (about 3 oz), coarsely grated, squeezed of excess moisture

½ cup (about 2 oz) coarsely grated Cheddar cheese (see tips)

3 tablespoons snipped chives

3 tablespoons olive oil

Cooked bacon, chopped avocado and baby spinach leaves, to serve

1 Whisk together the milk and egg yolks in a large bowl. Gradually whisk in the combined flours and baking powder until smooth and well incorporated. Stir through the corn, zucchini, cheese and chives.

2 Use an electric mixer with a whisk attachment to whisk the egg whites in a clean, dry bowl until stiff peaks form. Gently fold the egg whites into the batter until just combined.

3 Heat half the oil in a large nonstick skillet over medium-high heat. Pour ⅓ cup of mixture per fritter into the pan, to cook 2–3 fritters at a time. Cook for 3 minutes each side or until golden and cooked through. Transfer to a plate, cover loosely with foil and keep warm. Continue with the remaining batter to make 8 fritters, adding a little more oil to the pan as necessary.

4 Serve the fritters with cooked bacon, avocado and baby spinach.

TIPS You can substitute any type of cheese for the grated Cheddar, such as crumbled feta, ricotta or even goat's cheese.

Whisking the egg whites and adding them to the batter at the end results in a much lighter, less dense fritter.

* These flavorsome fritters make a wonderful brunch or light lunch.

Buckwheat griddle cakes with blueberries & sweet ricotta

PREPARATION TIME: 15 MINUTES
COOKING TIME: 10 MINUTES
MAKES ABOUT 22

2/3 cup buckwheat flour

1/2 cup all-purpose flour

1½ teaspoons baking powder

3 tablespoons sugar

2 eggs, separated

¾ cup buttermilk

2 teaspoons natural vanilla extract

8 oz (1 cup) fresh ricotta cheese

1½ tablespoons confectioners' or icing sugar mixture, sifted

Unsalted butter, for cooking

¾ cup (4 oz) fresh blueberries

* Buckwheat flour has quite a strong flavor, so when using it to make griddle cakes or flapjacks it is best to use some regular wheat flour as well.

1 Combine the flours, baking powder and sugar in a large bowl. Make a well in the center, add the egg yolks, buttermilk and half the vanilla and whisk until smooth. The batter will be quite stiff.

2 Use an electric mixer with a whisk attachment to whisk the egg whites in a clean, dry bowl until stiff peaks form. Gently fold the egg whites into the batter until just combined. The batter will be quite sticky now.

3 To make the sweet ricotta, put the ricotta, remaining vanilla and confectioners' sugar in a bowl and stir to combine. Set aside.

4 Heat a little butter in a nonstick skillet over medium-high heat. Drop tablespoonfuls of the mixture into the pan and cook for 1–2 minutes each side or until the griddle cakes are golden and cooked through. Transfer to a plate, cover loosely with foil and keep warm. Repeat with the remaining mixture, adding a little more butter to the pan as necessary.

5 Serve the griddle cakes topped with a teaspoon of sweet ricotta and a few blueberries.

TIP For a savory variation to serve as a canape, omit the sugar and serve topped with a little cream cheese and some thinly sliced smoked salmon.

Buckwheat, honey & nut granola bars

PREPARATION TIME: 15 MINUTES
COOKING TIME: 45–55 MINUTES
MAKES 16

2/3 cup honey

1/2 cup sunflower oil

1/4 cup firmly packed light brown sugar

2 1/2 cups rolled oats

1 cup puffed buckwheat

1/2 cup shredded coconut

1 teaspoon ground cinnamon

1/2 cup dried cranberries

1/2 cup coarsely chopped seedless raisins

1/2 cup raw cashew nuts, coarsely chopped

1 Preheat the oven to 275°F. Line a 9 x 13 inch baking tin with parchment paper.

2 Put the honey, oil and sugar in a medium saucepan over medium heat and cook, stirring, until the sugar has dissolved and the ingredients are well combined. Set aside.

3 Put the rolled oats, buckwheat, coconut, cinnamon, cranberries, raisins and nuts in a large bowl. Add the honey mixture and stir to combine. Using slightly wet hands, press the mixture firmly into the lined tin. Press the mixture with the back of a spoon to make the surface smooth and even.

4 Bake for 40–50 minutes or until the surface is dark golden brown all over. Cool completely in the tin before cutting into 16 bars.

TIPS For a gluten-free version, replace the oats with quinoa flakes.
  You can substitute puffed millet or amaranth for the puffed buckwheat if you prefer.
  These granola bars will keep in an airtight container for up to 5 days. For extra-crisp granola bars, store in an airtight container in the refrigerator.

✳ *Home-made granola bars are healthier and tastier than bought ones and you know exactly what is in them. I find that cooking them for a longer time at a lower temperature gives a crisp and golden result and you do not need to use as much oil or butter.*

Brown rice

NUTRITIONAL INFORMATION
(per 7 oz/1 cup cooked brown rice)

Energy: 913 kilojoules, 218 calories Protein: 4.5 g Total fat: 1.6 g

Saturated fat: 0.3 g Carbohydrate: 45.8 g Sugars: 1 g Dietary fiber: 3.5 g

Cholesterol: 0 mg Vitamin B$_6$: 0.3 mg Iron: 1.0 mg Magnesium: 84 mg

Manganese: 2.1 mg Phosphorus: 150 mg Sodium: 2 m

Gluten free

Rice was first cultivated in China, with records going back to about 2500 BC. Archaeological discoveries show that rice was even grown long before this, but in dry conditions rather than rice paddies. For the majority of its long history rice was a staple only in Asia, until traders and conquerors introduced it to all corners of the world. The majority of rice is still grown in Asia, where it is an important part of the food culture of those countries. Thailand, Vietnam and China are the three largest exporters of rice.

In Asia, brown rice is often referred to as 'rough' rice and it was traditionally rarely eaten except by the poor, the sick and the elderly. Nowadays the tables have turned and brown rice is valued for its higher nutritional value and is enjoying an emerging popularity.

Brown rice has a delicious nutty taste, a slightly chewy texture and a far superior nutrient profile than highly processed white rice. This is because brown rice is the whole grain, with only the inedible outer husk removed, and therefore it retains the nutrient-rich bran and germ. White rice is both milled and polished, which removes the bran layer and germ, and the nutrients they contain, particularly vitamins B_2 and B_3, iron and magnesium. Brown rice and white rice do have similar calorific (kilojoule) and carbohydrate values, however.

Brown rice is a great source of carbohydrates — in fact, 90 per cent of the kilojoule content of rice is due to carbohydrates. As brown rice is not as refined as white rice, it takes longer to digest and contains significantly more fiber, making you feel satisfied faster. Brown rice is an excellent source of the trace mineral manganese, and the minerals magnesium and selenium. One cup of cooked brown rice contains 84 mg magnesium, compared to just 19 mg in white rice.

Brown rice also contains phytochemicals, including phenolic acids, phytic acid, plant sterols and saponins. The bran in brown rice is high in insoluble dietary fiber.

Brown rice is most readily available in long-grain and medium-grain varieties. Long-grain brown rice is ideal to use in pilafs and warm or cold salads, where you want the grains to remain fluffy and separated. Medium-grain is a great all-purpose rice with a little more starch, so it can be used in stuffings for meat and vegetables, salads and even to make sushi. Short-grain is ideal for rice desserts and risotto, where you want a rich creamy texture. Brown rice risotto takes over an hour to cook, so I find baking it is the easiest method as it does not require constant stirring.

Brown rice flakes are ideal for making gluten-free porridge, they only take minutes to cook, so are great for a quick breakfast. Also, try adding rice bran flakes to home-made granola.

To cook brown rice

To cook by absorption, place 1 cup long- or medium-grain brown rice in a saucepan with $1\frac{1}{2}$ cups water and bring to a boil. Reduce the heat and simmer, covered, for 25–30 minutes or until the water has evaporated. Remove from the heat, keep covered and set aside for 5 minutes.

To boil, place the same amount of rice in a large saucepan, add 6 cups water and bring to a boil, stirring occasionally. Reduce the heat and boil gently, uncovered, for 25–30 minutes. Drain well.

Fried rice with Chinese sausage, egg & kecap manis

PREPARATION TIME: 15 MINUTES
COOKING TIME: 10 MINUTES
SERVES 4

2 tablespoons sunflower oil

3 eggs, lightly whisked

1 medium white onion, finely chopped

2 celery ribs, trimmed and diced

6 oz Chinese sausage (lap cheong, see tip), thinly sliced

1 long red chile, seeded and finely chopped

2 teaspoons finely grated ginger

4 cups cold cooked medium-grain brown rice (see page 75)

5 oz (1 cup) frozen green peas, thawed

3 tablespoons light soy sauce

1½ tablespoons kecap manis

4 scallions, trimmed and thinly sliced, to garnish

1 Heat 1 teaspoon of the oil in a large nonstick wok or skillet over medium heat. Pour half the whisked egg into the wok and swirl to cover the base. Cook for 1 minute or until set. Carefully loosen the edges, turn out onto a board and set aside to cool. Repeat with another teaspoon of oil and the remaining egg. Roll up both the omelets and cut into thin strips. Set aside.

2 Heat the remaining oil in the wok over high heat. Add the onion and celery and stir-fry for 2 minutes, then add the Chinese sausage and stir-fry for a further 2 minutes or until crisp. Add the chile and ginger and stir-fry for 30 seconds. Add the rice and peas and cook, tossing, for 2–3 minutes or until the rice is heated through. Add the soy sauce and kecap manis and toss to combine.

3 Serve the fried rice garnished with sliced omelet and scallions.

TIP Chinese sausage is a spiced dried pork sausage that can be found in the Asian section of supermarkets or from Asian grocers.

❋ Fried rice is an excellent way to use up leftover rice. This version contains almost seven times the amount of fiber than one based on white rice.

Lamb biryani with coconut & chile relish

PREPARATION TIME: 20 MINUTES
(+ 2–3 HOURS MARINATING)
COOKING TIME: 1 HOUR 30 MINUTES
SERVES 4

4 teaspoons ground cumin

4 teaspoons sweet paprika

1 teaspoon ground turmeric

¼ cup plain yogurt

1½ lb diced boneless lamb leg

1½ cups brown basmati
(or long-grain) rice

3 tablespoons sunflower oil

2 medium yellow onions, thinly sliced

2 cloves garlic, crushed

2 teaspoons finely grated ginger

3½ cups chicken broth (see tip)

Baby spinach leaves, plain yogurt and
lime wedges (optional), to serve

COCONUT & CHILE RELISH

2 long green chiles, seeded
and finely chopped

¼ cup coarsely chopped cilantro leaves

½ cup shredded coconut,
lightly toasted

3 tablespoons lime juice

½ teaspoon sugar

1 Put half each of the cumin, paprika and turmeric in a shallow glass or ceramic dish. Add the yogurt and stir to combine. Add the lamb and stir to coat, then cover with plastic wrap and place in the refrigerator for at least 2–3 hours to marinate. Soak the brown rice in a bowl of cold water for 1 hour, then rinse well in a sieve and drain.

2 Meanwhile, preheat the oven to 350°F. Heat 2 teaspoons of the oil in a large flameproof casserole dish over high heat. Cook the lamb, in batches, for 2–3 minutes or until golden, adding another 2 teaspoons of oil when necessary. Transfer to a bowl and set aside.

3 Reduce the heat to medium, add the remaining oil and the onions to the casserole dish and cook, stirring occasionally, for 5 minutes. Add the garlic, ginger and remaining spices and cook, stirring, for 2 minutes or until fragrant. Add the rice, stirring to coat in the spices. Add the broth and bring to a boil, then return the lamb to the dish in a single layer on top of the rice.

4 Cover the dish with a lid and bake for 1 hour 15 minutes or until the broth is absorbed and the lamb and rice are tender.

5 Meanwhile, to make the coconut & chile relish, combine all the ingredients in a medium bowl and season with sea salt and freshly ground black pepper, to taste.

6 Serve the biryani with the coconut & chile relish, baby spinach, yogurt and a wedge of lime, if desired.

TIP If you want this dish to be gluten free, make sure you use gluten-free broth.

Rice salad with roasted squash, beans & orange spice dressing

PREPARATION TIME: 25 MINUTES
COOKING TIME: 30 MINUTES
SERVES 4

5½ cups (1½–2 lb) winter squash, peeled, seeded and cut into ¾ inch cubes

1½ tablespoons olive oil

8 oz green beans, trimmed and cut into 1¼ inch lengths (about 3 cups)

3 cups cooked medium-grain brown rice (see page 75), cooled

1 medium zucchini, trimmed, halved and thinly sliced

¼ cup sunflower seeds

¼ cup flat-leaf parsley leaves, coarsely chopped

¼ cup mint leaves, shredded

ORANGE SPICE DRESSING
⅓ cup freshly squeezed orange juice

3 tablespoons olive oil

1 tablespoon white wine vinegar

1 teaspoon honey

½ teaspoon ground cinnamon

1½ teaspoons ground cumin

1 Preheat the oven to 400°F. Put the squash on a large baking sheet lined with parchment paper. Season with sea salt and freshly ground black pepper and drizzle with the olive oil. Roast for 25–30 minutes, until the squash is golden and tender.

2 Meanwhile, blanch the beans in a saucepan of boiling water until bright green and tender-crisp. Refresh under cold running water, then drain well.

3 Put the roasted squash, beans, rice, zucchini, sunflower seeds, parsley and mint in a large bowl and stir to combine.

4 To make the dressing, put all the ingredients in a small bowl and whisk to combine. Add to the salad and stir to combine. Season with sea salt and freshly ground black pepper, to taste.

TIP This salad will keep, covered, in the refrigerator for up to 2 days.

I love using brown rice in salads as it gives so much flavor and texture. It stays al dente even after the dressing is added.

SUSHI WITH SPICY
SESAME CHICKEN &
AVOCADO (PAGE 84)

Sushi with spicy sesame chicken & avocado

PREPARATION TIME: 30 MINUTES
(+ 1 HOUR MARINATING AND
30 MINUTES CHILLING)
COOKING TIME: 45 MINUTES
MAKES 4 LARGE ROLLS

1½ cups medium-grain or short-grain brown rice

¼ cup seasoned rice vinegar

¼ cup white vinegar

4 sheets nori

1 small cucumber, cut into ¼ x 2 inch batons

½ avocado, peeled, pit removed and cut into ¼ x 2 inch batons

Pickled ginger, wasabi and tamari (see tip), to serve

SPICY SESAME CHICKEN

¼ teaspoon dried red chile flakes

1 clove garlic, crushed

3 tablespoons tamari (see tip)

1½ tablespoons sesame oil

2 (about ½ lb in total) skinless boneless chicken thighs

❋ Brown rice takes longer to break down in your body than white rice, so this sushi will help your blood sugar levels remain stable throughout the day.

1 To make the spicy sesame chicken, put the chile flakes, garlic, tamari and sesame oil in a shallow glass or ceramic container. Add the chicken and stir to coat, then cover and put in the refrigerator for at least 1 hour to marinate.

2 Meanwhile, put the rice in a large saucepan with 3 cups cold water and bring to a boil over high heat. Reduce the heat to low, cover and simmer for 30–35 minutes, until all the water is absorbed. Remove from the heat, cover and set aside for 5 minutes.

3 Add the seasoned rice vinegar to the rice and stir until well combined. Cover a large baking sheet with foil, then spread the rice evenly over and set aside to cool completely.

4 Meanwhile, heat a chargrill pan or nonstick skillet over high heat and cook the chicken for 3–4 minutes each side, until golden and cooked through. Remove and set aside to cool, then cut into ½ inch thick slices.

5 Combine the white vinegar and 1 cup cold water in a small bowl. Divide the rice into 4 portions. Place a sheet of nori, shiny side down, on a bamboo mat. Dip your hands in the vinegar mixture, then use them to spread one portion of the rice evenly over the bottom two-thirds of the nori sheet, leaving a small border around the edge.

6 Place a few slices of chicken along the middle of the rice and top with some cucumber and avocado. Lift up the end of the mat closest to you and roll it over the ingredients to enclose, then keep rolling to make a complete roll. Continue with the remaining nori, rice and fillings. Wrap each roll tightly in plastic wrap and refrigerate for 30 minutes. Slice and serve with pickled ginger, wasabi and tamari.

TIP If you want this dish to be gluten free, make sure you use gluten-free tamari.

Brown rice porridge with vanilla baked rhubarb

PREPARATION TIME: 10 MINUTES
COOKING TIME: 15 MINUTES
SERVES 4

1½ cups milk (see tips)
½ teaspoon ground cinnamon
2 cups brown rice flakes

VANILLA BAKED RHUBARB
1–1½ lb rhubarb, trimmed and cut into 2 inch lengths (about 7 cups)
¼ cup sugar
½ cup freshly squeezed orange juice
1 teaspoon natural vanilla extract

* Compared to regular rice or brown rice, brown rice flakes take very little time to cook, so they are ideal for a quick breakfast. They are also a gluten-free alternative to traditional oat-based porridge and have a rich and creamy texture once cooked.

1 Preheat the oven to 350°F. To make the vanilla baked rhubarb, place the rhubarb in a single layer in a roasting pan, sprinkle with the sugar and drizzle with the orange juice and vanilla. Cover the pan with foil and bake for 10–15 minutes (check the rhubarb after 10 minutes), or until tender.

2 Meanwhile, put the milk, 2 cups water and the cinnamon in a large saucepan. Bring to a boil over medium heat.

3 Add the brown rice flakes to the pan and return to a boil, then reduce the heat to low and simmer, stirring, for 3–4 minutes or until thick and creamy. Serve topped with the rhubarb and any pan juices.

TIPS You can use any type of milk, such as soy or rice, in this recipe.
When rhubarb is out of season, you can try serving the porridge topped with fresh berries or sliced banana and a drizzle of maple syrup or honey.

Roasted pork loin with cumin, quince & pistachio stuffing

PREPARATION TIME: 25 MINUTES
(+ COOLING, AND 15 MINUTES RESTING)
COOKING TIME: 1 HOUR
SERVES 8

4–5 lb rolled boneless
pork loin (see tips)

1½ tablespoons olive oil

2 teaspoons sea salt

Steamed green beans, to serve

STUFFING

1½ tablespoons olive oil

1 large yellow onion, finely chopped

1 teaspoon ground cumin

1 teaspoon ground coriander

2 cups cooked medium-grain brown
rice (see page 75), cooled

4 oz quince paste, chopped

⅓ cup pistachios, chopped

3 tablespoons chopped flat-leaf parsley

1 Preheat the oven to 425°F. To make the stuffing, heat the olive oil in a skillet over medium heat and cook the onion, stirring occasionally, for 3–4 minutes or until softened. Add the spices and cook, stirring, for a further minute. Set aside.

2 Put the rice, onion mixture, quince paste, pistachios and parsley in a large bowl. Use clean hands to mix until combined (see tips). Season well with salt and pepper, then set aside to cool completely.

3 Unroll the pork loin and place, rind side up, on a board or clean work surface. Use a sharp knife to score the rind crossways at ¾ inch intervals. Turn the pork over and cut a vertical slit into the thick end of the fillet, going halfway through the meat. Pack the stuffing into the slit and along the center of the loin.

4 Starting at the thicker end, tightly roll up the pork to enclose the filling. Tie with kitchen string at ¾ inch intervals, then place the pork rind-side up in a large roasting pan. Drizzle with the oil and rub the salt into the rind.

5 Roast the pork for 25 minutes or until the rind crackles, then reduce the oven temperature to 350°F and roast for a further 45–50 minutes or until the rind is crisp and golden and a meat thermometer inserted into the thickest part of the meat reads 160°F. Transfer the pork to a plate (don't cover with foil) and set aside for 15 minutes to rest before slicing. Serve with green beans.

* *Whole grains such as brown rice are great to use in stuffings, as they absorb all the juices without becoming soggy. Middle Eastern flavors such as cumin, quince and pistachio complement the nutty flavor of the rice.*

TIPS For extra crisp and crunchy crackling, place the pork loin on a baking sheet, skin side up and uncovered, in the refrigerator overnight. You can ask your butcher to score the pork for you.

It is important to rub the quince paste evenly through the rice mixture, as it helps to make the rice stick together and this in turn makes it easier to stuff the pork.

You could use cooked pearl barley, buckwheat, millet or quinoa instead of the rice.

Cauliflower, rice & lentil salad with tahini dressing

PREPARATION TIME: 15 MINUTES
COOKING TIME: 15 MINUTES
SERVES 4

1–1½ lb cauliflower, trimmed and cut into florets (about 4 cups)

3 tablespoons olive oil

1 medium yellow onion, thinly sliced

2 teaspoons brown mustard seeds

2 teaspoons ground cumin

3 tablespoons dried currants

2 cups freshly cooked brown rice (see page 75)

1 can (approx. 14 oz) brown lentils, drained and rinsed

1½ tablespoons lemon juice

3 tablespoons chopped cilantro leaves, to garnish (optional)

TAHINI DRESSING

¼ cup Greek-style yogurt

1½ tablespoons tahini (see tip)

1½ tablespoons lemon juice

1 To make the tahini dressing, combine the yogurt, tahini and lemon juice in a small bowl. Mix in 2–3 tablespoons warm water, enough to make a dressing-like consistency. Set aside.

2 Blanch the cauliflower in a saucepan of boiling water for 3–4 minutes or until tender-crisp. Refresh under cold running water, then drain well.

3 Heat the oil in a large deep skillet over medium-high heat and cook the onion, stirring occasionally, for 3–4 minutes or until golden. Add the mustard seeds and cumin and cook, stirring, for 1 minute. Add the cauliflower and cook, stirring often, for a further 2–3 minutes, until the cauliflower is golden. Add a little extra oil to the pan if necessary.

4 Add the currants, rice and lentils to the pan and cook for 2 minutes or until heated through. Season with salt and freshly ground black pepper, then stir through the lemon juice. Serve the salad warm, drizzled with the tahini dressing and garnished with cilantro, if desired.

TIP Tahini is a Middle Eastern paste made from ground sesame seeds and olive oil. You can find it in the health food section of your supermarket. Check the label to make sure it is gluten free.

* *Whole grains and legumes are made for each other, as together they make a complete protein, which is especially important for vegetarians and vegans.*

Five-spice duck breast with ginger & scallion rice

PREPARATION TIME: 20 MINUTES
COOKING TIME: 20 MINUTES
SERVES 4

4 x 6 oz duck breast fillets, with skin

1½ tablespoons light brown sugar

½ teaspoon sea salt

1 teaspoon Chinese five-spice powder

4 oz (1½ cups) fresh shiitake mushrooms, sliced

1¼ inch piece ginger, peeled and julienned

6 scallions, trimmed and thinly sliced diagonally, plus extra, to garnish

7 oz snow peas, trimmed and thinly sliced (about 3 cups)

4 cups cooked brown rice (see page 75), cooled

3 tablespoons mirin (Japanese cooking wine)

1½ tablespoons tamari (see tip)

2 teaspoons sesame oil

1 Preheat the oven to 350°F. Use a sharp knife to score the skin of each duck breast 5–6 times. Combine the sugar, salt and five-spice. Rub the sugar mixture evenly into the skin of each duck breast.

2 Heat a large skillet over medium heat and cook the duck, skin side down, for 6–7 minutes, until the skin is crisp and the fat has rendered down. Turn and cook for a further minute. Transfer to a large baking sheet, skin side up, reserving 1 tablespoon of the rendered duck fat. Roast the duck for 5 minutes for medium, then transfer to a clean board. Cover loosely with foil and set aside for 5 minutes to rest.

3 Meanwhile, heat the reserved duck fat in a large wok over high heat. Add the mushrooms and stir-fry for 2 minutes, then add the ginger and scallions and stir-fry for 1 minute more. Add the snow peas and stir-fry for 1 minute, then add the rice, mirin, tamari and sesame oil and stir-fry for a further 2 minutes or until the rice is heated through.

4 Thinly slice the duck. Divide the rice among 4 serving bowls, top with slices of duck and garnish with the extra scallion.

TIP If you want this dish to be gluten free, make sure you use gluten-free tamari.

❋ This dish is quick to make and tastes amazing! Brown rice pairs well with the robust flavors of shiitake mushrooms and duck, and using the rendered duck fat to stir-fry the rice adds even more flavor to the dish.

Creamy coconut rice with caramelized strawberries

PREPARATION TIME: 10 MINUTES
COOKING TIME: 30 MINUTES
SERVES 4

3 cups cooked medium-grain brown rice (see page 75)

1 can (14 fl oz) low-fat coconut milk

¾ cup milk

½ cup (2 oz) grated palm sugar or jaggery (see tips)

1 cinnamon stick

CARAMELIZED STRAWBERRIES

½ lb strawberries, hulled and halved (about 1½ cups)

2 tablespoons sugar

1 Put the rice, coconut milk, milk, jaggery and cinnamon stick in a large saucepan over medium heat. Bring to a boil, then reduce the heat to low and simmer, stirring occasionally, for 20–25 minutes or until thick and creamy. Set aside to cool slightly (see tips).

2 When you are ready to serve, make the caramelized strawberries. Heat a large skillet over medium-high heat and add the strawberries and 2 teaspoons of water. Sprinkle the sugar evenly over the strawberries and cook, stirring occasionally, for 1–2 minutes or until the strawberries are slightly caramelized.

3 To serve, divide the creamy rice among serving glasses or bowls, and top with some caramelized strawberries and any pan juices.

TIPS Palm sugar or jaggery is a coarse, sticky sugar usually sold in hard cakes from Asian grocers and supermarkets.

This rice dessert can be served warm or at room temperature.

The trick to making a creamy brown-rice dessert is to cook the rice first, otherwise it can take over an hour of stirring!

For a vegan version, use soy, almond or rice milk.

❋ Although rice dessert is traditionally made with white rice, this brown-rice version has a delicious nutty flavor and is far higher in fiber.

Chia

NUTRITIONAL INFORMATION
(per ½ oz chia seeds)

Energy: 287 kilojoules, 68 calories Protein: 3.1 g Total fat: 4.9 g

Saturated fat: 0.5 g Omega 3 ALA: 3.2 g Omega 6 LA: 0.9 g

Carbohydrate: 0.2 g Sugars: <1 g Dietary fiber: 6.2 g Calcium: 107 g

Iron: 2.5 mg Magnesium: 59 mg Phosphorus: 160 mg Sodium: 0.3 mg

Gluten free

Chia

Chia is an annual herb belonging to the mint family, and is still grown today for its edible seeds. Chia is technically not a grain (like amaranth, quinoa and buckwheat), but deserves its place in this book due to its ancient history, its recent revival and more importantly its unique and amazing nutritional properties.

Originally from Southern Mexico and Guatemala, chia seeds were an important food source for the Aztecs and Mayans. During this time chia was not only eaten as a grain, but used in beverages, medicines, pressed for its oil and ground to be used in breads.

Chia seeds are tiny in appearance, similar in size to sesame or poppy seeds. They are small flat disks with a slightly mottled appearance. They vary in color from black to grey, brown and even white.

The most impressive quality of chia seeds is their omega 3 content. Chia seeds have the highest plant content of omega-3 fatty acids, which have a wide array of health benefits. These include cardiovascular health, cancer and diabetes prevention, relief from joint stiffness, assisting in depression treatment and even improved memory. Chia seeds are also a good source of omega-6 fatty acids.

Chia seeds are high in fiber, especially insoluble fiber, assisting in gastrointestinal health and reduced risk of colon cancer. Chia is also a rich protein source and contains all the essential amino acids, as well as several non-essential ones.

Chia is gluten free, so it is suitable for those with celiac disease, and it is also rich in several vitamins and minerals including calcium, iron, magnesium, phosphorus and potassium.

Chia is available as seeds and, less commonly, as chia oil or bran. Chia seeds have a variety of food uses — they can be eaten raw, sprinkled on salads, dips, roasted vegetables or over granola. They can be baked in muffins, granola bars, cookies, cakes and breads, or added to drinks such as smoothies. Chia seeds are mixed with water or fruit juice to make 'chia fresca' in Mexico.

Chia oil is produced by extracting the oil from chia seeds, and is a wonderful plant source of omega 3. The oil should not be heated as it will lose its nutritional value. It has a mild flavor, so is ideal to drizzle over salads or combine with olive oil in salad dressings. You can also add a teaspoon of the oil to a smoothie. Once opened, chia oil needs to be kept in the fridge.

Chia bran is the husk of the chia seed, and is extremely high in dietary fiber, containing both soluble and insoluble fiber, which assists with overall digestive health. It can be added to baked items such as muffins, to smoothies to give body or sprinkled over cereal.

Chia's versatility and ease of preparation make it extremely easy to incorporate into your diet. You also only need a relatively small serve to gain nutritional benefits.

To make chia gel

Add 1/3 cup chia seeds to 2 cups cold water in a large airtight container with a lid. Cover and shake the container until well combined, then set aside for 20–30 minutes or until a gel forms, shaking the container every 10 minutes. This mixture can keep, covered, in the fridge, for up to 2 weeks. Add it to drinks to give them a nutritional boost.

Chia, mango & raspberry breakfast smoothie

PREPARATION TIME: 5 MINUTES
COOKING TIME: NIL
SERVES 2

1½ cups milk

½ cup yogurt

2 tablespoons white chia seeds

1 ripe mango (about 13 oz), seed and skin removed, flesh diced

2 oz (½ cup) fresh or frozen raspberries

2 teaspoons honey

1 Put all the ingredients in a blender and blend until smooth. Serve immediately.

TIP If you prefer a smoother texture, you can make a gel from the chia seeds before adding to your smoothie. Put the chia seeds in a bowl with a pouring lip with 1 cup of water and set aside for 10 minutes or until a gel forms. Reduce the milk to ¾ cup and add the chia gel with the remaining ingredients.

* *Putting chia seeds in a smoothie adds one-eighth of an ounce of fiber per serving, as well as a good dose of omega-3 and omega-6 fatty acids.*

Roasted root vegetables with chia dukkah

PREPARATION TIME: 25 MINUTES
COOKING TIME: 45 MINUTES
SERVES 4

6 medium beets (about 1½ lb in total), peeled and cut into wedges

2 large parsnips (about 14 oz in total), peeled and cut into thick batons

1 large bunch baby carrots (about 1 lb in total), trimmed, scrubbed and halved lengthways if large

3 tablespoons olive oil, plus extra, to drizzle

CHIA DUKKAH

4 teaspoons coriander seeds

4 teaspoons cumin seeds

½ cup pistachios, lightly toasted

3 tablespoons white chia seeds

2 teaspoons sea salt

1 Preheat the oven to 400°F. Put the vegetables in a single layer on a large baking sheet lined with parchment paper. Drizzle with the olive oil and season with sea salt and freshly ground black pepper. Roast the vegetables for 40–45 minutes or until tender.

2 Meanwhile, to make the chia dukkah, put the coriander and cumin seeds in a small dry skillet over medium-high heat. Cook, stirring, for 2–3 minutes or until fragrant. Transfer to a mortar and pestle and pound until finely crushed.

3 Put the toasted spices, pistachios, chia seeds and salt in a small food processor and process until finely chopped.

4 To serve, pile the roasted vegetables onto a serving platter, sprinkle with the chia dukkah and drizzle with a little extra olive oil.

TIP The dukkah will keep, stored in an airtight container, for up to 1 month. Try sprinkling it over broiled meats (such as lamb chops, chicken or beef) or broiled pita or flat bread as part of a mezze plate.

* *Chia seeds work just like sesame seeds in this delicious dukkah. They also add dietary fiber, essential fatty acids and protein. Just add a leafy salad, goat's cheese and a slice of bread to make this a complete meal, or serve as a warm vegetable side.*

Smoked chicken, chia & broccolini salad with chile sesame dressing

PREPARATION TIME: 15 MINUTES
COOKING TIME: 5 MINUTES
SERVES 4

2 bunches broccolini (about 1 lb in total), trimmed and cut into long florets

2 x 6–7 oz smoked chicken breasts (see tips), skin removed and thinly sliced

1 firm ripe avocado, peeled, pit removed and cut into thin wedges

Approx 2 cups (4 oz) baby spinach leaves

1½ tablespoons black chia seeds

DRESSING

2 teaspoons sesame oil

2 tablespoons mirin (Japanese cooking wine)

1½ tablespoons olive oil

1½ tablespoons tamari (see tips)

1½ tablespoons rice wine vinegar

1 long red chile, seeded, finely chopped

* A really simple way to include chia in your diet is to sprinkle the seeds over fresh salads. As chia does have gelling properties once added to liquid, this is best done just before serving.

1 To make the dressing, put all the ingredients in a small bowl and whisk to combine. Set aside.

2 Blanch the broccolini in a large saucepan of boiling water until bright green and tender-crisp. Refresh under cold running water, then drain well.

3 Put the broccolini, chicken, avocado and spinach leaves in a large bowl and gently toss to combine.

4 Divide the salad among 4 serving bowls, drizzle with a little of the dressing and sprinkle with the chia seeds.

TIPS You can replace the smoked chicken breasts with two 6–7 oz broiled chicken breasts, thinly sliced, or 2 cups shredded skinless barbecued chicken.

If you want this dish to be gluten free, make sure you use gluten-free smoked chicken breasts and tamari.

Chia-crusted salmon with Asian greens & tamari dressing

PREPARATION TIME: 10 MINUTES
COOKING TIME: 10 MINUTES
SERVES 4

3 tablespoons white chia seeds

3 tablespoons black chia seeds

4 x 6 oz skinless salmon fillets

2 bunches choy sum (1 lb 9–12 oz), washed and trimmed

3 tablespoons sunflower oil

1¼ inch piece ginger, peeled and julienned

2 cloves garlic, thinly sliced

Noodles (see tip) or steamed brown rice, to serve

TAMARI DRESSING

3 tablespoons oyster sauce (see tip)

3 tablespoons tamari (see tip)

1½ tablespoons Chinese rice wine

1 teaspoon sugar

1 Combine the white and black chia seeds on a plate. Press each salmon fillet in the chia seeds to evenly coat one side, then set aside.

2 Remove the stems from the choy sum, cut in half if long and reserve. To make the tamari dressing, put all the ingredients in a small bowl and stir to dissolve the sugar.

3 Heat 1 tablespoon of the oil in a large nonstick skillet over high heat. Cook the salmon, chia side down, for 2–3 minutes or until golden. Turn and cook for a further 2 minutes (for medium) or until cooked to your liking. Set aside and keep warm.

4 Meanwhile, heat the remaining oil in a large wok or skillet over high heat. Add the ginger and garlic and stir-fry for 30 seconds. Add the choy sum stems and stir-fry for 1–2 minutes, then add the choy sum leaves and stir-fry for 1 minute more or until almost wilted. Add half the dressing and toss to combine.

5 To serve, divide the choy sum among serving plates, top each with a piece of salmon and drizzle over a little of the remaining dressing. Serve with noodles or steamed rice.

TIP If you want this dish to be gluten free, make sure you use gluten-free noodles, oyster sauce and tamari.

* Chia seeds are a great alternative to bread crumb crusts for those on a gluten-free diet.
Chia seeds, the highest plant source of omega fatty acids, and salmon ensure this meal is packed with essential fatty acids. Asian greens are rich in vitamins A, C and K, and are a good source of potassium and calcium.

Chargrilled asparagus with lemon & garlic dressing

PREPARATION TIME: 15 MINUTES
COOKING TIME: 5 MINUTES
SERVES 4

2 bunches asparagus (about 10 oz in total), trimmed
1½ tablespoons olive oil
1½ tablespoons black chia seeds

DRESSING
1½ tablespoons chia oil
1½ tablespoons olive oil
1½ tablespoons lemon juice
1 teaspoon finely grated lemon zest
1 clove garlic, crushed

1 To make the dressing, put all the ingredients in a small bowl and whisk to combine. Set aside.

2 Preheat a chargrill pan or barbecue grill plate on high. Drizzle the asparagus with the olive oil and cook for 2–3 minutes, turning, or until lightly charred and tender-crisp.

3 Transfer the asparagus to a serving plate, drizzle with the dressing and season with sea salt and freshly ground black pepper. Sprinkle with the chia seeds and serve immediately.

* *Chia oil is an excellent plant source of omega-3 fatty acids, which have a wide array of health benefits. These include cardiovascular health, cancer and diabetes prevention, relief from joint stiffness and improved memory.*

Unlike other sources of omega-3 fatty acids, such as fish oil, chia oil has a mild flavor so is ideal to add to salad dressings.

CHIA CREPES WITH
STAR ANISE MANDARINS
(PAGE 110)

Chia crepes with star anise mandarins

PREPARATION TIME: 20 MINUTES
(+ 1 HOUR CHILLING)
COOKING TIME: 25 MINUTES
SERVES 4

¾ cup all-purpose flour

1 teaspoon sugar

1 egg, lightly whisked

1 cup milk

1½ tablespoons butter, melted,
plus extra, for greasing

3 tablespoons black chia seeds

Greek-style yogurt, to serve

STAR ANISE MANDARINS

⅔ cup sugar

1 cinnamon stick

2 star anise

3 medium seedless mandarins
(see tips), peeled, white pith
removed and segmented

Chia seeds don't just make these crepes look fantastic visually, they also add texture.

1 Sift the flour into a large bowl and stir through the sugar and a pinch of salt. Add the egg, milk and melted butter and whisk until smooth. Refrigerate for at least 1 hour.

2 Meanwhile, to make the star anise mandarins, put the sugar, cinnamon stick and star anise in a medium saucepan with ⅔ cup water. Cook, stirring, over medium heat to dissolve the sugar, then bring to the boil. Reduce the heat and simmer, without stirring, for 5 minutes or until syrupy. Add the mandarin segments and simmer for 2 minutes, then remove from the heat and set aside to cool.

3 Heat a medium nonstick skillet over medium heat and brush the pan with a little extra butter. Stir the chia seeds into the batter (see tips). Ladle ¼ cup batter into the pan and tilt the pan slightly to quickly and evenly spread it out. Cook for 1 minute, then lift the outer edge and flip it over. Cook for a couple of seconds on the other side, then transfer to a plate and keep warm. Repeat with the remaining batter to make 8 crepes.

4 To serve, fold each crepe into quarters and place 2 crepes on each serving plate. Top with a dollop of yogurt and spoon over some of the mandarins and syrup. Serve immediately.

TIPS You can replace the yogurt with heavy cream or even mascarpone cheese for a more decadent dessert.

When mandarins are out of season, substitute 3 large navel oranges, peeled, white pith removed and segmented.

It is important to add the chia seeds to the batter just before you begin cooking the crepes, due to their gelling properties.

Chia seed Italian cookies

PREPARATION TIME: 20 MINUTES
COOKING TIME: 20 MINUTES
MAKES 36

2 egg whites, at room temperature

1 cup superfine sugar

1 cup ground almonds

2/3 cup chopped milk chocolate, or chocolate chips (see tips)

1/2 cup black chia seeds

1/2 cup sesame seeds

* *These more-ish little cookies are packed with fiber and good oils. They're the perfect thing to have with a coffee or cup of tea. Or, try crumbling them and layering in short glasses with cream and berries for a simple and delicious dessert.*

1 Preheat the oven to 275°F. Line 2 large baking sheets with parchment paper.

2 Use an electric mixer with a whisk attachment to whisk the egg whites in a large bowl until firm peaks form. With the motor running, gradually add 1/2 cup of the sugar, a spoonful at a time, whisking until it is dissolved. Combine the ground almonds and the remaining sugar. Fold the almond mixture, chocolate, chia and sesame seeds through the egg white mixture.

3 Spoon 2 teaspoonfuls of the mixture per biscuit onto the lined trays, leaving 1 1/2 inches between each to allow for spreading. Bake for 20 minutes, swapping the baking sheets halfway through cooking, or until just golden and crisp. Remove and set aside on the baking sheets to cool completely.

TIPS If you want these cookies to be gluten free, make sure you use gluten-free chocolate.

Keep in an airtight container for up to 1 week.

Chia, banana & chocolate muffins

PREPARATION TIME: 15 MINUTES
COOKING TIME: 20 MINUTES
MAKES 12

2 cups self-rising flour (see tips)

3 tablespoons black chia seeds

½ cup shredded coconut

⅔ cup sugar

1 cup (9 oz) mashed banana

7 tablespoons unsalted butter, melted and cooled

½ cup milk

⅔ cup chopped milk chocolate or chocolate chips

1 Preheat the oven to 350°F. Brush a 12-cup (⅓ cup) muffin tin with melted butter to grease or line with paper liners.

2 Sift the flour into a large mixing bowl and stir through the chia seeds, coconut and sugar. Combine the banana, melted butter and milk, add to the dry ingredients and stir to combine — do not overmix. Fold through the chopped chocolate.

3 Divide the mixture among the prepared muffin cups and bake for 20 minutes or until golden and cooked through. Set aside for 5 minutes to cool slightly, then transfer to a wire rack to cool.

TIPS If you do not have self-rising flour, substitute 2 cups all-purpose flour, 2 teaspoons baking powder and ½ teaspoon salt.

These muffins can be frozen for up to 1 month, wrapped well in plastic wrap. Thaw at room temperature.

* *Add chia seeds to baked goods such as muffins, cakes and cookies as you would sesame seeds or poppy seeds for extra dietary fiber and omega-3 fatty acids.*

Chia, date & walnut slice

PREPARATION TIME: 10 MINUTES
(+ CHILLING)
COOKING TIME: NIL
MAKES 16 WEDGES

1½ cups rolled oats

¾ cup walnut halves

½ cup shredded coconut

¼ cup white or black chia seeds

1 teaspoon ground cinnamon

1½ tablespoons unsweetened cocoa powder, sifted

2 teaspoons natural vanilla extract

15 oz pitted dried dates, chopped (about 2½ cups)

Pure confectioners' or icing sugar, to serve

1 Put the oats, walnuts, coconut, chia seeds, cinnamon, cocoa and vanilla in a food processor and process until all the ingredients are finely chopped.

2 With the motor running, start adding the dates a few pieces at a time, processing until all the dates have been added and the mixture is starting to come together. Use clean hands to bring it together completely, adding 1–2 teaspoons of cold water if necessary.

3 Press the mixture evenly into a round 8 inch cake pan, smoothing the surface firmly with the back of a metal spoon. Cover and refrigerate until ready to serve.

4 To serve, dust with confectioners' sugar and cut into thin wedges.

TIP This slice will keep, covered with plastic wrap, in the refrigerator for up to 2 weeks.

* *This slice is easy to make, wheat free and satisfies sweet cravings perfectly, making it a perfect snack or after-dinner treat with coffee.*

Millet

NUTRITIONAL INFORMATION
(per 6 oz/1 cup cooked millet)

Energy: 867 kilojoules, 207 calories Protein: 6.1 g Total fat: 1.7 g

Saturated fat: 0.3 g Carbohydrate: 41.2 g Sugars: 0.2 g

Dietary fiber: 2.3 g Cholesterol: 0 mg Iron: 1 mg Phosphorus: 174 mg

Magnesium: 77 mg Manganese: 0.5 mg Sodium: 3.5 mg

Gluten free

Millets

Millets are a group of small, round seeded cereal grains thought to have originated in western Africa. They have been important food staples throughout human history and have been cultivated in East Asia for the last 10,000 years. In fact, these ancient grains predate wheat and rice as a cultivated grain.

Because they can grow in harsh environments where other grain crops do not grow well, millets are a major food source in arid and semi-arid regions of the world, including India and Africa, where millet flour, sometimes mixed with sorghum flour, is made into a flat bread (roti). In 2009, some 26 million tons of millet were produced around the world, with India and Nigeria being the largest producers.

Millet also features in the traditional cuisine and cultures of many other countries — millet porridge, sweetened with milk and sugar, is a traditional food in Russia; candied millet puffs are a speciality of Osaka, Japan; 'tongba' is a millet-based alcoholic brew in Nepal; millet is boiled with apples and honey in Germany; and in China millet is made into soup or mixed with brown sugar and used by nursing mothers to aid in milk production.

Nutritionally, millet is gluten free and suitable for those with celiac disease or other forms of allergies/intolerances to wheat. It is also easy to digest and was traditionally used to feed the sick, but as it is a mild thyroid peroxidase inhibitor it should not be consumed in great quantities by those with thyroid disease.

Millet is a good source of manganese and contains a moderate amount of dietary fiber. It also contains the minerals phosphorus, zinc, copper and various phytochemicals including lignans, phenolic acids, phytic acid, plant sterols and saponins.

Millet is available as millet grain (hulled), millet meal, puffed millet and millet flour. The grains are tiny and are similar in appearance to yellow mustard seeds. They have a mild, buttery, slightly corn-like taste, and toasting the grain before cooking helps bring out this flavor.

Millet works beautifully with ingredients such as lime, chile, herbs and spices. It can be used in salads instead of rice, quinoa or couscous, in pilafs, as a breakfast cereal, added to soups and stews and even to make a polenta-like dish. Once cooked it does retain quite an *al dente* texture, and the grains do separate on standing.

Millet meal can be used in baked goods as you would use polenta, and it has a similar texture. It is delicious combined with ground almonds in a gluten-free cake.

Puffed millet is ideal to add to home-made granola or baked goods such as granola bars.

Millet flour can be used in flat breads that do not require leavening, or it can replace some of the wheat flour in cakes and cookies. It gives a distinct golden color and buttery taste to baked goods.

To cook millet

Heat a large saucepan over medium-high heat, add 1 cup hulled millet and cook, stirring, for 3 minutes or until fragrant. Add 2 cups water and bring to the boil. Reduce the heat to low, cover and simmer for 20 minutes or until the water is absorbed. Remove from the heat and set aside, still covered, to steam for 10 minutes. Fluff the grains with a fork and transfer to a large bowl to cool completely.

NOTE Sometimes you may find you need to add an extra 1/2 cup water during cooking.

Millet salad with chile lime shrimp

PREPARATION TIME: 20 MINUTES
(+ COOLING)
COOKING TIME: 40 MINUTES
SERVES 4

½ teaspoon dried red chile flakes

2 teaspoons finely grated lime zest

3 tablespoons olive oil

20 raw large shrimp, peeled and deveined with tails left intact

1 cup hulled millet

2 large ears sweetcorn

1 bunch (about 5 oz) asparagus, trimmed and halved

1 firm ripe avocado, peeled, pit removed and diced

½ cup cilantro leaves, coarsely chopped

Lime wedges, to serve

DRESSING

3 tablespoons lime juice

3 tablespoons olive oil

1 long red chile, seeded and finely chopped

½ teaspoon sugar

1 Put the chile flakes, lime zest and 1 tablespoon of the olive oil in a shallow glass or ceramic bowl. Add the shrimp and stir to coat, then cover and set aside.

2 Heat a large saucepan over medium-high heat, add the millet and cook, stirring, for 3 minutes or until fragrant.

3 Add 2 cups water to the millet and bring to the boil. Reduce the heat to low, cover and simmer for 15–20 minutes or until the water is absorbed. Remove from the heat and set aside, covered, to steam for 10 minutes. Fluff the grains with a fork and transfer to a large bowl to cool completely.

4 Heat a large chargrill pan over high heat. Drizzle the corn and asparagus with the remaining oil. Cook the corn, turning, for 6–8 minutes or until lightly charred and tender. Remove and set aside to cool slightly, then cut the kernels from the ears. Cook the asparagus and shrimp for 2 minutes each side or until the asparagus is tender-crisp and the shrimp are just cooked through. Set the shrimp aside. Add the asparagus, corn kernels, avocado and cilantro to the millet.

5 To make the dressing, put all the ingredients in a small bowl and whisk until well combined and the sugar is dissolved. Add to the salad and toss gently to combine. Season with sea salt and freshly ground black pepper, to taste.

6 To serve, divide the salad among serving plates, top with the chargrilled shrimp and serve with lime wedges.

* *Buttery and almost corn-like, millet is a good match with Mexican flavors such as lime, chile and cilantro.*

Millet is relatively quick to cook, is gluten free and has an al dente *texture once cooked.*

Creamy parmesan millet with ratatouille

PREPARATION TIME: 20 MINUTES
COOKING TIME: 50 MINUTES
SERVES 4

1 cup hulled millet

2 cups chicken or vegetable broth (see tips)

2/3 cup (3 oz) finely grated Parmesan cheese, plus coarsely grated Parmesan, to serve

RATATOUILLE

3 tablespoons olive oil

1 medium red onion, diced

2 cloves garlic, crushed

1 red bell pepper, seeded and cut into 3/4 inch dice

2 medium zucchini, trimmed and cut into 3/4 inch dice

1 small eggplant, trimmed and cut into 3/4 inch dice

1 can (14 oz) chopped tomatoes

2 teaspoons thyme leaves

1 Heat a large saucepan over medium-high heat, add the millet and cook, stirring, for 3 minutes or until fragrant.

2 Add the broth and 2 cups water to the millet and bring to the boil over high heat. Reduce the heat to low, cover and simmer, stirring occasionally, for 45 minutes or until thick and creamy. Add a little extra water during cooking if it looks too dry. Stir through the Parmesan and season with sea salt and freshly ground black pepper.

3 Meanwhile, to make the ratatouille, heat the olive oil in a large pan over medium heat. Add the onion and cook, stirring occasionally, for 5 minutes or until softened. Add the garlic and cook, stirring, for 1 minute more.

4 Increase the heat to high, add the bell pepper, zucchini and eggplant and cook, stirring occasionally, for 5 minutes or until the vegetables are golden. Add the tomatoes and thyme, reduce the heat to low and simmer for 10 minutes or until the vegetables are tender, adding a little water if the sauce is becoming too thick. Season with sea salt and freshly ground black pepper, to taste.

5 To serve, divide the Parmesan millet among 4 shallow bowls, top with some ratatouille and sprinkle with the coarsely grated Parmesan.

TIPS If you want this dish to be gluten free, make sure you use gluten-free broth.

You can also make millet porridge using the same method. Simply toast the millet as in step 1 and then follow step 2, replacing the broth with water. Omit the Parmesan and serve with a drizzle of honey and a little milk.

✻ When I first heard millet could be used to make a soft polenta-like dish, I was skeptical. However, I could not believe the end result — creamy, rich and best of all, unlike polenta it does not become stiff on standing. The trick is to cook it slowly with a higher ratio of liquid than usual.

Millet-stuffed roast chicken

PREPARATION TIME: 20 MINUTES
(+ COOLING)
COOKING TIME: 1 HOUR 20 MINUTES
SERVES 4

3 tablespoons olive oil

1 small yellow onion, finely chopped

5 oz sliced uncooked bacon (about 3 slices, see tips), rind removed, diced

2 cloves garlic, crushed

1 cup cooked millet (see page 119)

3 tablespoons coarsely chopped parsley

1½ tablespoons finely chopped sage

1 teaspoon finely grated lemon zest

3–4 lb free-range chicken

Roast potatoes and steamed greens, to serve

1 Heat 1 tablespoon of the oil in a large skillet over medium-high heat. Add the onion and bacon and cook, stirring occasionally, for 5 minutes or until golden. Add the garlic and cook, stirring, for 1 minute more. Transfer the mixture to a large bowl and add the millet, herbs and lemon zest. Season with sea salt and freshly ground black pepper, then set aside to cool.

2 Preheat the oven to 425°F. Rinse the chicken and pat dry with kitchen paper. Spoon the stuffing into the cavity of the chicken. Tie the legs together with kitchen string.

3 Place the chicken, breast side up, in a large roasting pan. Drizzle with the remaining olive oil and season with salt and pepper. Roast for 20 minutes, then reduce the oven temperature to 400°F and cook for a further 50 minutes or until the juices run clear when you prick the thickest part of the thigh. (Cover the chicken with foil if it is browning too quickly.)

4 Remove the chicken from the oven and set aside for 10 minutes to rest before carving. Serve with roast potatoes and steamed greens.

TIPS If you want this dish to be gluten free, make sure you use gluten-free bacon.

I think millet works particularly well with poultry or pork, so you could also try this stuffing in spatchcock, quail, turkey or a rolled pork loin.

Millet works wonderfully as a stuffing, as it absorbs the flavors and juices from the chicken. It is also a gluten-free alternative to a traditional bread crumb stuffing. Using millet in a stuffing is a great way to introduce it to people, as they won't know it's in there but will enjoy the flavor.

Millet, fava beans & peas with marinated feta

PREPARATION TIME: 15 MINUTES
(+ COOLING)
COOKING TIME: 30 MINUTES
SERVES 4

1 cup hulled millet

1 lb (about 3 cups) fresh or frozen fava beans

6 oz (1 cup) shelled fresh green peas

3 oz (1 cup) pea shoots

3 tablespoons snipped chives

4 oz marinated feta cheese, drained and crumbled

2 preserved lemon quarters, flesh and white pith removed, thinly sliced

DRESSING

3 tablespoons olive oil (see tip)

3 tablespoons lemon juice

Pinch of sugar

1 Heat a large saucepan over medium-high heat, add the millet and cook, stirring, for 3 minutes or until fragrant.

2 Add 2 cups water to the millet and bring to the boil. Reduce the heat to low, cover and simmer for 15–20 minutes or until the water is absorbed. Remove from the heat and set aside, covered, for 10 minutes to steam. Fluff the grains with a fork and transfer to a large bowl to cool completely.

3 Blanch the fava beans and peas in a saucepan of boiling water for 2–3 minutes or until tender-crisp. Refresh under cold running water, then drain well. Peel away and discard the outer skins from the fava beans.

4 Add the peas, fava beans, snow pea shoots, chives and half the feta to the millet and stir to combine. To make the dressing, put the olive oil, lemon juice and sugar in a small bowl and whisk to combine.

5 Add the dressing to the salad and toss to combine. Season with sea salt and freshly ground black pepper, to taste. Serve topped with the remaining feta and sprinkled with the preserved lemon.

TIPS Try using some of the oil from the feta jar in the dressing — it is usually olive oil combined with garlic and herbs and will add extra flavor to your salad.

Any leftovers can be kept in an airtight container in the refrigerator for lunch the following day.

* *This salad makes a great accompaniment to broiled meats or seafood. To make it a complete (balanced) meal, you could flake a hot-smoked salmon fillet into the salad or add a handful of nuts.*

Toasting the millet before cooking really brings out its buttery, corn-like flavor.

MILLET, SPINACH &
CASHEW PILAF WITH LAMB
CHOPS (PAGE 130)

Millet, spinach & cashew pilaf with lamb chops

PREPARATION TIME: 20 MINUTES

COOKING TIME: 35 MINUTES

SERVES 4

1 cup hulled millet

1½ tablespoons olive oil, plus extra, to brush

1 medium yellow onion, finely chopped

2 cloves garlic, crushed

1½ tablespoons korma curry paste (see tips)

2 cups chicken broth (see tips)

8 lamb chops or a rack of lamb cut into 8 chops and french trimmed

Approx 2 cups (4 oz) baby spinach leaves

¼ cup cashew nuts, lightly toasted, coarsely chopped

3 tablespoons dried currants

1½ tablespoons lemon juice

Greek-style yogurt, to serve

> * *I love to use millet in pilafs instead of white rice, as it has so much more flavor and retains its texture. In comparison to white rice, millet has over twice as much fiber and almost twice as much protein!*

1 Heat a skillet over medium-high heat, add the millet and cook, stirring, for 3 minutes or until fragrant. Remove from the heat.

2 Heat the olive oil in a large heavy-bottomed saucepan over medium heat. Cook the onion, stirring occasionally, for 5 minutes or until softened. Add the garlic and curry paste and cook, stirring, for 1 minute or until fragrant.

3 Add the toasted millet and broth and bring to the boil. Reduce the heat to low, cover and simmer for 25 minutes or until the liquid is absorbed. Remove from the heat and set aside, covered, for 10 minutes to steam.

4 Meanwhile, heat a large chargrill pan over high heat. Brush the chops with a little extra oil and cook for 2 minutes each side or until lightly charred and cooked to your liking.

5 Stir the spinach leaves, cashews, currants and lemon juice through the pilaf and season with sea salt and freshly ground black pepper, to taste. Divide the pilaf among serving plates and top each with 2 lamb chops. Serve with a dollop of yogurt.

TIPS You can use any Indian-style curry paste in this recipe.
   If you want this dish to be gluten free, make sure you use gluten-free curry paste and broth.

Healing chicken & millet soup

PREPARATION TIME: 20 MINUTES
COOKING TIME: 2 HOURS 20 MINUTES
SERVES 4

3–4 lb free-range chicken

1 large yellow onion, coarsely chopped

1 large carrot, peeled and coarsely chopped

3 celery ribs, trimmed and chopped

10 black peppercorns

3 flat-leaf parsley stalks

2 teaspoons olive oil

1 medium leek, trimmed, white part only, halved and thinly sliced

1/3 cup hulled millet

Snipped chives, to garnish

* *This soup is both soothing and nurturing, the perfect food for when you are unwell. Millet is historically known for its therapeutic uses, as it is gluten free and very easily digested.*

1 Rinse the cavity of the chicken and place in a large saucepan with the onion, carrot, celery, peppercorns and parsley. Add enough cold water to just cover the chicken and slowly bring to the boil over high heat. Reduce the heat to low, skim any scum and oil that comes to the surface and simmer for 1 hour. Carefully remove the chicken and set aside to cool slightly. Return the broth to the heat and simmer for a further 30 minutes.

2 Strain the broth, discarding the solids, and set aside. When the chicken is cool enough to handle, remove the skin and bones and shred the breast meat (see tips). Set aside.

3 Place a large clean saucepan over medium heat and add the olive oil and leek. Cook, stirring occasionally, for 5–6 minutes or until softened. Add 6 cups of the reserved broth (see tips). Add the millet and simmer for 30 minutes or until tender. Add the shredded chicken and simmer for a further 5 minutes. Season with sea salt and freshly ground black pepper, to taste. Serve garnished with chives.

TIPS The rest of the chicken meat can be shredded and used to make chicken sandwiches or added to salads.

Any remaining broth can be frozen and used to make risotto, sauces or soup.

This soup is suitable to freeze.

Orange & almond syrup cake

PREPARATION TIME: 30 MINUTES
(+ COOLING)

COOKING TIME: 45–50 MINUTES

SERVES 10–12

¾ cup unsalted butter, at room temperature

1¼ cups superfine sugar

4 eggs

1 cup millet meal

1 tablespoon baking powder (see tips)

2½ cups ground almonds

2 teaspoons finely grated orange zest

Greek-style yogurt, to serve

SYRUP

1 medium orange, plus ½ cup freshly squeezed orange juice

½ cup sugar

* I like to use millet meal in cakes where I would typically use polenta. Polenta and millet are both gluten free, but I prefer the texture of millet meal because it is not as coarse.

1 Preheat the oven to 350°F. Grease a round 8½ inch springform cake pan and line the base and side with parchment paper.

2 Use an electric mixer to beat the butter and sugar until pale and creamy. Add the eggs one at a time, beating well after each addition. Fold in the millet meal, baking powder, ground almonds and orange zest until well combined.

3 Spoon the mixture into the prepared pan and smooth the surface with the back of the spoon. Bake for 45–50 minutes, covering the top of the cake with foil after 30 minutes, or until a skewer inserted into the center comes out clean. Remove and set aside to cool for 10 minutes, then carefully remove the side of the pan and transfer to a wire rack over a metal tray.

4 Meanwhile, to make the syrup, finely grate the zest of the orange (reserve the orange). Put the zest, juice and sugar in a small saucepan and cook, stirring, over low heat until the sugar has dissolved. Increase the heat to high and bring to the boil, then reduce the heat and simmer for 2 minutes.

5 Remove the syrup from the heat and carefully brush half the syrup over the warm cake, then set aside to cool completely. Brush the cake with the remaining syrup. Use a small sharp knife to remove the white pith from the orange and cut the flesh into segments. Serve the cake with the yogurt and orange segments.

TIPS If you want this cake to be gluten free, make sure you use gluten-free baking powder.

Try adding a few drops of orange blossom water to the orange syrup for a Middle Eastern flavor.

To make small individual cakes, line a 12-cup muffin tin with paper liners. Divide the mixture among the lined muffin cups and bake for 20 minutes or until cooked through.

Crystallised ginger millet cookies

PREPARATION TIME: 25 MINUTES

COOKING TIME: 15 MINUTES

MAKES ABOUT 24

½ cup unsalted butter, at room temperature

½ cup firmly packed light brown sugar

⅓ cup golden syrup

1 cup millet flour

¾ cup all-purpose flour

4 teaspoons ground ginger

1 teaspoon ground cinnamon

⅓ cup crystallized ginger, finely chopped, plus ¼ cup extra, to garnish

1 Preheat the oven to 350°F. Line 2 large baking sheets with parchment paper.

2 Use an electric mixer to beat the butter, sugar and golden syrup in a large bowl until pale and creamy. Sift the millet flour, all-purpose flour, ground ginger and cinnamon together, add to the butter mixture with the crystallized ginger and stir until well combined.

3 Roll tablespoons of the mixture into balls and place on the lined baking sheets, leaving 1½ inches between each to allow for spreading. Flatten the balls slightly with clean fingers, then garnish with a little extra crystallized ginger. Bake for 12–15 minutes, turning the baking sheets halfway through cooking, or until the cookies are golden.

4 Cool the cookies on the baking sheets for 10 minutes before transferring to a wire rack to cool completely.

TIP Keep in an airtight container for up to 1 week.

* These cookies remind me of old-fashioned ginger snaps, but they are so much better! They are crisp on the outside, but still a little chewy in the center. The millet flour gives a buttery flavor and adds to their golden color.

Oats

NUTRITIONAL INFORMATION
(per 9 oz/1 cup rolled oats cooked in water)

Energy: 695 kilojoules, 166 calories Protein: 5.9 g

Total fat: 3.6 g Saturated fat: 0.7 g Carbohydrate: 31.8 g

Sugars: 0.6 g Dietary fiber: 4.0 g Cholesterol: 0 mg

Iron: 2.1 mg Magnesium: 63.2 mg Manganese: 1.4 mg

Phosphorus: 180 mg Selenium: 12.6 mg Sodium: 9.4 mg

Oats draw their ancestry from the wild red oat, a plant originating in the Near East. They have been cultivated for more than 2000 years in various regions throughout the world, particularly Europe where they were a dietary staple in many countries, including Great Britain, Germany and Scandinavia. Scottish settlers introduced oats to North America in the 1600s.

Although oats are a familiar food to many people, most do not realize just how nutritious they are. Simple, economical and easy to source, oats and oat products can be used not only for porridge and granola, but an amazing array of dishes.

After harvesting, oats are roasted, cleaned and hulled. This process does not remove the bran and germ, which are a concentrated source of fiber and nutrients.

Oats contain more soluble fiber than any other grain, including beta-glucans, a type of soluble fiber that has been proven to help lower cholesterol and therefore possibly reduce the risk of heart attack.

The soluble fiber and protein content of oats also results in slower digestion and an extended sensation of fullness. So if you eat oats for breakfast you may find you eat less food throughout the rest of the day.

Oats can also help reduce blood sugar and insulin levels, so can be of assistance in controlling diabetes. Oats contain iron, manganese, zinc, vitamin E, folate, B vitamins, phosphorus and selenium. They also contain antioxidants that are beneficial for health such as avenanthramides, phenolic acids and phytic acid.

Oats can be found in various forms, as groats (kernels), steel-cut oats, rolled oats, quick oats, instant oats, oat bran and oat flour. Oats become thick and creamy when cooked with liquid due to their high soluble fiber content and are naturally a little sweet, making them the perfect addition to baked goods.

Oat groats are the whole oat kernels that have not been flattened in any way. They can be used in salads as you would barley or spelt, and are available from health food stores. Steel-cut oats are groats that have been sliced and they have a chewy texture, ideal for using in porridge or cereal, although they're harder to find than rolled oats.

The rolled oats that are commonly available are stabilized, that is, steamed and then rolled, with a flatter shape than steel-cut oats. Their soft texture makes them ideal for granola, baking, porridge and as a coating for meat or fish. Unstabilized rolled oats are not steamed before they are rolled, so they are slightly more nutritious but have a shorter shelf life as they turn rancid quickly. As a result, they can be quite hard to find. (In North America, they are sold as 'raw rolled oats'.) Quick oats are steamed, finely cut and rolled, making them quicker to cook and with a softer texture than rolled oats. Instant oats are similar to quick oats but often have flavorings added.

Oat bran is the outer husk of an oat grain and is rich in fiber, vitamins and minerals. It is great to add to baked goods such as bread, muffins, cookies, smoothies and as a substitute for bread crumbs in meatloaf or burgers. Oat flour is made from ground whole oats and can be used when making breads and other baked goods.

To cook oats

Place 1 cup rolled oats in a medium saucepan with 2 cups cold water and bring to the boil. Reduce the heat to low and simmer, stirring occasionally, for 5 minutes or until thick and creamy.

Bircher muesli with blackberries & almonds

PREPARATION TIME: 15 MINUTES
(+ OVERNIGHT SOAKING)
COOKING TIME: NIL
SERVES 4

2 cups rolled oats

1½ cups apple juice

½ cup milk

1 cup Greek-style yogurt

1 large apple, peeled, cored and coarsely grated

½ cup raw almonds, chopped

3 tablespoons sunflower seeds

Fresh blackberries, to serve

Honey, to drizzle

1 Put the oats, apple juice and milk in a medium bowl and stir to combine. Cover and refrigerate overnight.

2 The next morning, add the yogurt, apple, three-quarters of the almonds and the sunflower seeds and stir to combine. Divide among serving bowls and top with blackberries, the remaining almonds and a drizzle of honey.

TIPS Try substituting the blackberries with fresh or thawed frozen blueberries or raspberries.

Keep, covered, in the refrigerator for up to 3 days.

* *Oats make a fantastic breakfast as they are high in fiber and have a low GI, so they release energy slowly throughout the day. Bircher muesli is a great way to incorporate oats into your breakfast regime, especially in the warmer months when you may not feel like porridge.*

Roasted sweet potato, zucchini & feta burgers

PREPARATION TIME: 20 MINUTES
(+ 20 MINUTES COOLING)
COOKING TIME: 30 MINUTES
SERVES 4

1 lb sweet potatoes (about 2), peeled and cut into ¾ inch dice

1 teaspoon ground cumin

3 tablespoons olive oil

1 medium zucchini, trimmed and coarsely grated

½ cup rolled oats, plus ⅔ cup, extra

4 oz creamy feta cheese, crumbled

¼ cup pine nuts, lightly toasted

3 tablespoons snipped chives

1½ tablespoons finely chopped flat-leaf parsley

⅓ cup hummus (store bought or homemade), to serve

4 wholegrain bread rolls, split and toasted, to serve

Baby romaine lettuce leaves and sliced tomato, to serve

1 Preheat the oven to 400°F. Line a large baking sheet with parchment paper. Place the sweet potato on the lined baking sheet in a single layer and sprinkle with the cumin, then drizzle with 1 tablespoon of the olive oil and season with salt and pepper. Roast for 25 minutes or until golden and tender. Transfer to a large bowl, roughly mash and set aside to cool.

2 Squeeze the excess moisture from the zucchini, then add to the sweet potato with the oats, feta, pine nuts and herbs. Season with sea salt and freshly ground black pepper. Using clean hands, mix until well combined and then shape into 4 patties. Place the extra oats on a large plate and press each patty into the oats to cover on all sides.

3 Heat the remaining olive oil in a large nonstick skillet over medium heat. Cook the patties for 3 minutes each side or until golden and crisp.

4 To serve, spread a little hummus on the base of each roll and top with lettuce, tomato and a patty. Cover with the tops of the rolls and serve immediately.

TIP Roasting the sweet potato is worth the extra effort as it gives much more flavor than steaming it. It also reduces the moisture content, resulting in a firmer burger that should not fall apart.

> *These veggie burgers are packed with flavor and the oats make a lovely crisp coating. They are an excellent source of dietary fiber and a good source of protein and unsaturated fatty acids.*

Lamb koftas with tzatziki, pita bread & cucumber salad

PREPARATION TIME: 20 MINUTES
(+ 30 MINUTES SOAKING)
COOKING TIME: 8 MINUTES
SERVES 4

1 lb ground lamb

¼ cup oat bran

1 egg

1 small red onion, grated

¼ cup pine nuts, lightly toasted and chopped

½ teaspoon dried mint

¼ teaspoon dried red chile flakes

1 teaspoon ground cumin

1½ tablespoons olive oil

Warmed pita bread and tzatziki, to serve

CUCUMBER SALAD

2 small cucumbers, peeled, halved lengthways, seeded and sliced

6 small radishes, trimmed and thinly sliced

¼ cup coarsely chopped flat-leaf parsley

1½ tablespoons olive oil

1½ tablespoons lemon juice

> * Oat bran is a good substitute for bread crumbs and it has the added bonus of being higher in dietary fiber. Look for it in the cereal section of the supermarket.

1 Soak 12 small wooden skewers in cold water for 30 minutes.

2 Put the ground lamb, oat bran, egg, onion, pine nuts, dried mint, chile flakes and cumin in a medium bowl and use clean hands to mix until well combined. Season with sea salt and freshly ground black pepper. Divide the mixture into 12 portions, then use slightly wet hands to shape each into a sausage shape around a soaked skewer. Set aside.

3 To make the cucumber salad, put the cucumber, radishes and parsley in a large bowl. Drizzle with the olive oil and lemon juice, toss to combine and season with salt and pepper, to taste.

4 Preheat a large chargrill pan or barbecue over high heat. Drizzle the koftas with the olive oil and cook, turning occasionally, for 6–8 minutes or until golden and cooked through.

5 Divide the koftas and cucumber salad among 4 plates and serve with warmed pita bread and tzatziki.

TIPS You could replace the lamb with ground beef or even pork. To make this a wheat-free meal, simply omit the pita bread.

Pork, veal, prune & prosciutto terrine

PREPARATION TIME: 20 MINUTES
(+ COOLING)
COOKING TIME: 40 MINUTES
SERVES 6

1½ tablespoons olive oil

1 medium yellow onion, finely chopped

1 medium carrot, peeled and
coarsely grated

1 small zucchini, trimmed and
coarsely grated

2 cloves garlic, crushed

1 teaspoon ground allspice

1–1½ lb ground mixed pork and veal

½ cup quick oats

⅓ cup chopped pitted dried prunes

⅓ cup pistachios

1 egg

10 thin slices prosciutto

1 Preheat the oven to 350°F. Spray a 3 inch deep, 4 x 8 inch loaf pan with olive oil.

2 Heat the olive oil in a large skillet over medium heat. Cook the onion, carrot and zucchini, stirring occasionally, for 5–6 minutes or until softened. Add the garlic and allspice and cook, stirring, for 1 minute. Transfer to a large mixing bowl and set aside to cool.

3 Add the ground pork and veal, oats, prunes, pistachios and egg and season with salt and pepper. Using clean hands, mix the ingredients until well combined.

4 Arrange the prosciutto slices over the base and 2 long sides of the pan, allowing them to overhang the sides. Spoon the meat mixture into the prosciutto-lined pan, pressing down firmly. Fold over the overhanging prosciutto to enclose the filling.

5 Cover with foil and bake for 15 minutes, then remove the foil and bake for a further 20 minutes or until firm to touch and the juices run clear when tested with a skewer. Remove from the oven and set aside for 10 minutes, then remove from the pan and cut into thick slices to serve.

TIP Serve this terrine warm with steamed vegetables or salad for dinner, or cold with arugula and relish for a delicious lunch.

✳ Quick oats can be used as a binding agent in recipes such as burgers, terrines and meatloaf, instead of bread crumbs. I like to add some grated vegetables as well – sneaking in a few extra veggies is always a good thing, and it reduces the amount of meat required, too.

Chicken & leek pies with crunchy oat topping

PREPARATION TIME: 30 MINUTES
COOKING TIME: 45 MINUTES
SERVES 4

1½ tablespoons olive oil

1½ tablespoons butter

1½ lb skinless boneless chicken breasts, cut into ¾ inch dice

2 medium leeks, white part only, thinly sliced

1 celery rib, trimmed and diced

2 cloves garlic, crushed

⅓ cup white wine

3 tablespoons all-purpose flour

½ cup chicken broth

⅓ cup light cream (18% MF)

5 oz (1 cup) frozen green peas, thawed

3 tablespoons snipped chives

Green salad or steamed greens, to serve

TOPPING

¾ cup rolled oats

¼ cup all-purpose flour

½ cup (2 oz) finely grated Parmesan cheese

3 tablespoons finely chopped flat-leaf parsley

¼ cup chilled unsalted butter, diced

1 Preheat the oven to 375°F. Lightly butter four 1-cup ovenproof baking dishes.

2 Heat the oil and butter in a large, deep skillet over high heat. Cook the chicken, in batches, for 2–3 minutes or until golden. Transfer to a plate and set aside.

3 Return the pan to medium heat and add the leeks and celery. Cook, stirring occasionally, for 5–6 minutes or until softened. Add the garlic and cook for 1 minute more. Return the chicken to the pan, add the wine and simmer until it has almost evaporated. Add the flour and cook, stirring, for 1 minute.

4 Add the broth and cream to the pan and simmer for 5 minutes or until thickened. Stir through the peas and chives and season with sea salt and freshly ground black pepper, to taste. Divide among the buttered dishes.

5 To make the topping, put the oats, flour, Parmesan, parsley and a large pinch of salt in a medium bowl. Use clean fingertips to rub in the butter until the mixture resembles small clumps.

6 Sprinkle the topping evenly over the pies. Bake for 20–25 minutes or until golden. Remove and set aside for 5 minutes to cool slightly before serving with a green salad or steamed greens.

TIP You could make one large pie if you wanted to — use a 4-cup ovenproof pie dish and bake the pie for 25–30 minutes.

Lemon, herb & oat crumbed fish

PREPARATION TIME: 20 MINUTES
(+ 30 MINUTES CHILLING)
COOKING TIME: 6 MINUTES
SERVES 4

1½ cups rolled oats

3 tablespoons finely chopped
flat-leaf parsley

3 tablespoons finely chopped dill

2 teaspoons finely grated lemon zest

½ cup all-purpose flour

2 eggs, lightly whisked

4 x 6 oz firm white fish fillets
(such as halibut or cod)

3 tablespoons olive oil

Mixed salad and lemon wedges,
to serve

1 Combine the oats, herbs and lemon zest in a shallow bowl. Place the flour in a second shallow bowl and the egg in a third.

2 Dust a piece of fish in the flour, then dip in the egg and finally press into the oat mixture until evenly coated. Place on a tray and repeat with the remaining fish. Cover and refrigerate for 30 minutes.

3 Heat the oil in a large nonstick skillet over medium-high heat (see tip). Cook the fish for 2–3 minutes each side or until golden and cooked through, adding a little more oil to the pan if necessary. Serve the fish with a mixed salad and lemon wedges.

TIP Make sure the heat isn't too high or the oats may burn.

* Oats are a fabulous alternative to bread crumbs for a healthy crumbed fish. They stick well and turn an enticing golden brown when pan-fried.

RHUBARB, HONEY & OAT
MUFFINS (LEFT, PAGE 152)
AND OAT, PARMESAN &
THYME CRACKERS (PAGE 153)

Rhubarb, honey & oat muffins

PREPARATION TIME: 20 MINUTES
COOKING TIME: 20 MINUTES
MAKES 12

1½ cups self-rising flour (see tips)

1 teaspoon ground cinnamon

**1½ cups quick oats, plus
2 tablespoons, extra**

**⅓ cup firmly packed light brown sugar,
plus 2 teaspoons, extra**

1 egg

⅓ cup honey

1 teaspoon natural vanilla extract

**7 tablespoons unsalted butter,
melted and cooled**

1 cup buttermilk

4 oz thinly sliced rhubarb (about 1 cup)

** Quick oats are smaller and
have a softer texture than regular
oats, resulting in lighter muffins.*

1 Preheat the oven to 350°F. Line a 12-cup muffin tin with paper liners.

2 Sift the flour and cinnamon into a large bowl. Stir through the oats and sugar. Whisk the egg, honey, vanilla, butter and buttermilk together in a large jug, add to the dry ingredients and stir until just combined. Stir through the rhubarb (do not overmix). Divide the mixture among the lined muffin cups.

3 Combine the extra oats and brown sugar, and sprinkle over the tops of the muffins. Bake for 20 minutes or until golden brown. Set aside for 5 minutes to cool slightly, then transfer to a wire rack to cool completely.

TIPS If you do not have self-rising flour, substitute 1½ cups all-purpose flour, 1½ teaspoons baking powder and ½ teaspoon salt.

These muffins freeze well, so make an extra batch and keep some in the freezer for a delicious breakfast on the run or to pack in lunch boxes.

Oat, parmesan & thyme crackers

PREPARATION TIME: 25 MINUTES
(+ 30 MINUTES CHILLING)
COOKING TIME: 25 MINUTES
MAKES ABOUT 30

1 cup oat bran

1 cup all-purpose flour

¼ teaspoon baking powder

3 tablespoons light brown sugar

1½ tablespoons chopped thyme leaves

⅔ cup (3 oz) finely grated Parmesan cheese, plus ¼ cup (1 oz), extra

7 tablespoons chilled unsalted butter, diced

1 egg yolk

¼ cup iced water

1 Preheat the oven to 350°F. Line 2 large baking sheets with parchment paper.

2 Put the oat bran, flour, baking powder, a large pinch of salt and the sugar in a food processor and pulse to combine. Add the thyme, Parmesan and butter and process until the mixture resembles fine bread crumbs. Add the egg yolk and water and process until the mixture comes together.

3 Divide the dough into 2 equal portions and shape each into a flat disk. Cover with plastic wrap and refrigerate for 30 minutes.

4 Use a lightly floured rolling pin to roll out a portion of dough on a lightly floured work surface until ¼ inch thick. Use a round 2 inch cutter to cut the dough into disks, re-rolling and cutting the scraps to make more disks, and place on the lined tray, 1¼ inches apart. Sprinkle with a little extra Parmesan and bake for 12 minutes or until light golden. Remove and set aside to cool completely on the trays. Repeat with the remaining dough.

TIPS These crackers make a great addition to a cheese platter. Try them with quince paste and blue cheese or vintage Cheddar.
Keep in an airtight container for up to 1 week.

* Oat bran is the outer husk of the oat grain and contains most of the grain's dietary fiber. Add it to cookies, crackers or muffins, sprinkle it over cereal or add it to smoothies for a simple way to increase fiber in your diet. Oat bran can be found in the cereal section of the supermarket.

Pear, strawberry & ginger crumble

PREPARATION TIME: 20 MINUTES
(+ 5–10 MINUTES COOLING)
COOKING TIME: 25–30 MINUTES
SERVES 6

2–2½ lb firm ripe pears
(about 10 medium), peeled,
cored and quartered

1½ tablespoons lemon juice

½ lb strawberries, hulled and halved
(about 1½ cups)

3 tablespoons sugar

1 teaspoon finely grated ginger

1½ tablespoons all-purpose flour

Vanilla ice cream or cream, to serve

CRUMBLE

½ cup rolled oats

½ cup shredded coconut

⅓ cup all-purpose flour

1 teaspoon ground ginger

⅓ cup firmly packed light brown sugar

6 tablespoons chilled unsalted
butter, diced

1 Preheat the oven to 350°F. Lightly grease six 1-cup ovenproof dishes with melted butter.

2 Thinly slice the pears, place in a large mixing bowl with the lemon juice and toss to combine. Add the strawberries, sugar, ginger and flour and toss to coat. Spoon the filling into the buttered dishes.

3 To make the crumble, put the oats, coconut, flour, ginger and sugar in a large mixing bowl. Use clean fingertips to rub in the butter until the mixture resembles small clumps. Sprinkle the crumble mixture evenly over the filling in each dish.

4 Cover the dishes with foil and bake for 15 minutes, then remove the foil and bake for a further 10–15 minutes or until the topping is golden and the pears are tender. Remove from the oven and set aside for 5–10 minutes to cool before serving with ice cream or cream.

TIPS You can substitute the rolled oats with rolled barley or spelt.
　To make one large crumble, use a 6-cup ovenproof baking dish and bake for 20–25 minutes, covering the dish with foil if the topping is browning too quickly.

* *This crumble is quick and easy to make, as the filling does not require precooking. If your pears are not ripe, they may take a little longer to cook. Simply cover the dish with foil if the topping starts becoming too golden during the extra cooking time.*

Cranachan with raspberries & honey

PREPARATION TIME: 15 MINUTES
(+ COOLING)
COOKING TIME: 5 MINUTES
SERVES 4

1 cup rolled oats

3 tablespoons light brown sugar

¾ cup heavy cream

1 cup Greek-style yogurt

¼ cup honey, plus extra, to drizzle (optional)

2 cups (9 oz) fresh raspberries

2–3 tablespoons whisky

1 Preheat the broiler on high. Spread the oats over a baking sheet in a single layer and sprinkle evenly with the sugar. Grill for 3 minutes, stirring occasionally, or until just golden (watch carefully to ensure they do not burn). Remove and set aside to cool.

2 Use an electric mixer with a whisk attachment to whisk the cream until soft peaks form. Fold through the yogurt, honey, half the raspberries and three-quarters of the cooled oats. Add the whisky, to taste, and gently fold in.

3 Spoon the mixture into four small, about ¾ cup, serving glasses, and top with the remaining raspberries and oats. Drizzle with a little extra honey, if desired.

> * *Cranachan is a traditional Scottish dessert of toasted oats, cream, whisky and often raspberries. I like to use a combination of cream and thick yogurt for a slightly less rich version. Toasting the oats first brings out their delicious nutty flavor.*

Spelt & Kamut

NUTRITIONAL INFORMATION
(per 7 oz/1 cup cooked spelt)

Energy: 1030 kilojoules, 246 calories Protein: 10.7 g Total fat: 1.6 g

Saturated fat: 0 g Carbohydrate: 51.3 g Sugars: 0 g Dietary fiber: 7.6 g

Cholesterol: 0 mg Niacin: 5.0 mg Iron: 3.2 mg Thiamin: 0.2 mg

Magnesium: 95.1 mg Manganese: 2.1 mg Phosphorus: 291 mg Sodium: 9.7 mg

NUTRITIONAL INFORMATION
(per 6 oz/1 cup kamut flour)

Energy: 2345 kilojoules, 558 calories Protein: 22.6 g Total fat: 4.8 g

Saturated fat: 0.96 g Carbohydrate: 94.4 g Sugars: 2.6 g Sodium: 12.3 mg

Accredited and extensive nutritional analysis
for kamut is limited due to its small production
and relatively recent availability.

Spelt

Spelt (*Triticum spelta*) is an ancient grain with a long and complex history dating back thousands of years in both Europe and the Middle East. It was one of the first grains used to make bread, and is mentioned in the Old Testament as well as various Roman texts. It was a staple grain with symbolic importance in ancient civilizations such as Greece and Rome.

As populations migrated, spelt became increasingly popular in Europe up until the end of the 1800s. However, when new developments in farming practices allowed common wheat to be harvested in a single process, spelt production dropped off. Its tough outer husk still required further processing and this made it less popular. It wasn't until the 1980s in Europe that spelt finally experienced a rebirth, and it was then introduced to North America.

Spelt is rich in vitamins B_2 and B_3, dietary fiber, manganese, phosphorus, niacin, thiamin and copper. Spelt also contains more protein, fats and crude fiber than common wheat.

Kamut

Kamut is the trademarked name for an ancient heirloom grain whose original name is khorasan. The exact history of khorasan is a little unclear, but we do know it originated in areas around Egypt. Elaborate stories exist about its origins, such as its presence in the tombs of Egyptian pharaohs, but they are a little dubious!

Kamut is a large grain that is higher in protein than common wheat, as well as several vitamins and minerals including selenium, magnesium and zinc.

Today, consumption of spelt and kamut is once again growing rapidly as people are becoming aware of the amazing nutritional benefits of these ancient grains. Spelt and kamut are both relatives of the common wheat grain, but their properties are quite different. Even though they are members of the wheat family, they can often be tolerated by those with wheat sensitivity.

Spelt and kamut are whole grains, containing all three parts of the grain: the bran, germ and endosperm. This is unlike wheat, as processing usually removes the bran and germ. Spelt and kamut therefore contain a wider range of nutrients than common wheat.

Spelt is available in its hulled whole-grain form (often called berries), as rolled flakes and a flour, which can be used in many of the same ways as wheat flour. Kamut is a little harder to find than spelt, and is available in its hulled whole-grain form and as a flour.

Spelt or kamut grain can be used in salads as you would use rice, pearl barley or couscous.

Products using spelt or kamut flour such as pasta and bread are now readily available and are becoming increasingly popular. Both spelt and kamut flour can be used for bread making, and each makes a highly nutritious loaf. Spelt has a delicious nutty flavor, whereas kamut has quite a rich buttery taste. Bread products made with spelt or kamut flour require a little less water and less kneading than regular wheat flour.

Spelt or kamut flour can be substituted or added to other baked goods such as muffins, pancakes and cookies. Spelt or kamut pasta is a great alternative to wholemeal (whole-wheat) pasta and both are ideal for pasta salads, teaming beautifully with ingredients such as pine nuts, basil, olives and vine-ripened tomatoes to name a few.

To cook spelt and kamut

To prepare spelt or kamut grain, place 1 cup grain in a saucepan with 6–8 cups water. Bring to the boil, then reduce the heat and simmer for 45–50 minutes or until the grains are *al dente*. Rinse under cold running water, then drain well.

Home-made pizzas with salami, tomato, red onion & arugula

PREPARATION TIME: 25 MINUTES
(+ 10 MINUTES STANDING
AND 1 HOUR RISING)
COOKING TIME: 20–25 MINUTES
MAKES 4 PIZZAS

⅓ cup tomato sauce

4 oz thinly sliced salami

2 large vine-ripened tomatoes, diced

1 small red onion, thinly sliced

6 oz fresh baby mozzarella balls
(bocconcini), thinly sliced

Approx 2 cups (4 oz) baby arugula
leaves, to serve

Balsamic vinegar, to drizzle (optional)

PIZZA DOUGH

1 teaspoon honey

3 cups spelt flour

1 cup tepid water

2 teaspoons (⅛ oz) dried yeast

2 tablespoons olive oil,
plus extra, to grease

** Kamut and spelt flour are
both great to use in baked goods
where you would typically use
wheat flour, such as cakes, breads
and pizza bases. They do contain
gluten; however, the gluten does
not require as much kneading as
regular wheat flour.*

1 To make the dough, put the honey, ½ cup of the flour and the water in a small bowl and whisk to combine. Sprinkle with the yeast and set aside for 10 minutes, until bubbling and foamy.

2 Put the remaining flour and a pinch of salt in a large bowl and add the yeast mixture and olive oil. Stir with a wooden spoon to combine, then use your hands to bring the mixture together to form a ball.

3 Turn the dough out onto a lightly floured work surface and knead for 3–4 minutes or until it is smooth and elastic. Take care not to over-knead the dough. Lightly grease a large bowl, put the dough in it and spread a little extra oil over the top of the dough to prevent a crust forming. Cover with plastic wrap and leave to rise in a warm, draught-free place for 1 hour or until the dough has doubled in size.

4 Preheat the oven to 450°F. Brush 2 large pizza trays with oil. Punch the dough down with your fist, then divide it into 4 equal portions. Set 2 portions aside, covered with a damp dish towel. Roll out the remaining portions of dough to make two 10–12 inch circles. Place each one on a greased tray.

5 Spread each pizza with 1½ tablespoons of tomato sauce, then top each with one-quarter of the salami, tomatoes and onion.

6 Bake the pizzas for 5 minutes, top each with one-quarter of the cheese, then return to the oven (swapping the trays around to ensure even cooking) and cook for 5–7 minutes more or until the toppings are golden and the bases are crisp. While they are cooking you can prepare the next 2 pizzas if you like. Remove the cooked pizzas from the oven and serve topped with arugula and a drizzle of balsamic, if desired. When you are ready, cook the next 2 pizzas, adding the cheese after 5 minutes of cooking, as before.

TIP For a vegetarian pizza try cubes of roasted squash with thinly sliced zucchini, crumbled fresh ricotta cheese and chopped parsley.

Warm spelt salad with roast tomato & eggplant

PREPARATION TIME: 20 MINUTES
COOKING TIME: 45 MINUTES
SERVES 4

1 cup spelt

1 medium eggplant, trimmed and cut into ¾ inch dice

1 large zucchini, trimmed and cut into ¾ inch dice

1 teaspoon ground cumin

¼ cup olive oil

1²/₃ cups (½ lb) cherry tomatoes, halved

½ cup basil leaves, torn

½ cup flat-leaf parsley leaves, coarsely chopped

4 oz creamy feta cheese, crumbled

3 tablespoons balsamic vinegar

1 Preheat the oven to 350°F. Cook the spelt in a large saucepan of lightly salted boiling water for 45 minutes or until *al dente*. Rinse under cold running water, then drain well.

2 Meanwhile, put the eggplant and zucchini on a large baking sheet lined with parchment paper in a single layer. Sprinkle with the cumin, drizzle with 1 tablespoon of the olive oil and season with sea salt and freshly ground black pepper. Roast for 12 minutes, then add the tomatoes to the baking sheet, cut side up. Roast the vegetables for a further 8–10 minutes or until the eggplant is tender and the tomatoes are just wilted.

3 Put the spelt, roasted vegetables, basil, parsley and feta in a large bowl and season with salt and pepper.

4 Combine the remaining 3 tablespoons of the olive oil and the balsamic vinegar, add to the salad and gently toss to combine.

TIP You could use kamut, pearl barley, brown rice, buckwheat or quinoa instead of the spelt, though the cooking times will vary.

* Spelt is ideal to use in salads where you would usually use rice, couscous or pasta. It works beautifully with Mediterranean flavors such as tomatoes, basil and balsamic vinegar.

Kamut pasta with honey-roasted squash, ricotta & crisp sage

PREPARATION TIME: 20 MINUTES

COOKING TIME: 25 MINUTES

SERVES 4

1½ tablespoons honey

3 tablespoons olive oil

½ teaspoon dried red chile flakes

5½ cups (1½–2 lb) butternut squash, peeled, seeded and cut into ½ inch dice

14 oz kamut pasta (we used penne)

1½ tablespoons unsalted butter

3 cloves garlic, very thinly sliced

16 small sage leaves

8 oz (1 cup) fresh ricotta cheese, crumbled

* *Kamut pasta is available from health food stores, delicatessens and gourmet supermarkets. It has a nutty taste that works well with the sweetness of the honey and squash in this dish. It also holds its shape well once cooked.*

1 Preheat the oven to 400°F. Combine the honey, 1 tablespoon of the olive oil and the chile flakes. Place the squash on a large baking sheet lined with parchment paper in a single layer. Season with sea salt and freshly ground black pepper, drizzle with the honey mixture and roast for 20–25 minutes or until it is golden and tender.

2 Meanwhile, cook the pasta in a large saucepan of lightly salted boiling water according to the packet instructions or until *al dente*. Drain well and return to the pan.

3 Heat the butter and remaining olive oil in a large skillet over medium-high heat. Add the garlic and sage leaves and cook, stirring, for 2 minutes or until the butter and garlic are light golden and the sage is crisp.

4 Add the squash, sage mixture and half the ricotta to the pasta and toss to combine. Season with salt and pepper, to taste. Serve the pasta topped with the remaining ricotta.

TIP Tossing half the ricotta through the hot pasta gives it a creamy consistency, without the fat that cream would bring. If the pasta is a little dry, try adding a little of the pasta's cooking liquid.

SEEDED SPELT BREAD
(PAGE 170)

Seeded spelt bread

PREPARATION TIME: 20 MINUTES
(+ 1 HOUR 30 MINUTES RISING)
COOKING TIME: 35 MINUTES
MAKES 1 LOAF (12–14 SLICES)

1½ tablespoons honey
1½ cups white spelt flour
1¼ cups tepid water
2 teaspoons (⅛ oz) dried yeast
1½ cups whole-wheat spelt flour
1 teaspoon sea salt
1½ tablespoons sesame seeds
1½ tablespoons flaxseeds
1½ tablespoons poppy seeds,
plus extra, to sprinkle
3 tablespoons rolled oats,
plus extra, to sprinkle
1½ tablespoons olive oil,
plus extra, to grease

* Spelt and kamut flour are ideal for bread making, as they are higher in nutrients (especially protein) than regular wheat flour and they have a surprisingly light texture when baked. Their nutty, slightly sweet flavor is similar to a light rye bread.

1 Put the honey, ½ cup of the white spelt flour and the water in a small bowl and whisk to combine. Sprinkle with the yeast and set aside for 10 minutes, until the mixture is bubbling and foamy.

2 Sift the remaining white spelt flour, the whole-wheat flour and the salt into a large bowl, then return the bran in the strainer to the bowl. Stir through the sesame seeds, flaxseeds, poppy seeds and oats. Add the yeast mixture and olive oil. Stir with a wooden spoon to combine, then use your hands to bring the mixture together to form a ball, adding a little more water if necessary.

3 Turn the dough out onto a lightly floured work surface and knead for 3–4 minutes or until smooth and elastic. Lightly grease a large bowl, put the dough in it and spread a little extra oil over the top of the dough to prevent a crust forming. Cover with plastic wrap and leave to rise in a warm, draught-free place for 1 hour or until the dough has doubled in size.

4 Preheat the oven to 350°F. Brush a 4 x 8 inch loaf pan with oil. Punch the dough down with your fist, shape into a 8 inch log and place in the oiled pan. Cover loosely with plastic wrap and set aside in a warm, draught-free place until doubled in size, about 20 minutes. Sprinkle the top with the extra poppy seeds and oats.

5 Bake the bread for 30–35 minutes or until it is golden brown and the loaf sounds hollow when tapped. (Cover the loaf loosely with foil if the top is browning too quickly.) Remove from the pan and set aside on a wire rack to cool.

TIPS You can use all whole-wheat spelt flour instead of the combined white and whole-wheat flour, but it will result in a slightly denser loaf.

Unlike regular wheat flour, it is important not to overknead the dough as the gluten will start to break down.

Chargrilled olive & anchovy yogurt flat breads

PREPARATION TIME: 20 MINUTES
(+ 20 MINUTES RESTING)
COOKING TIME: 25 MINUTES
MAKES 6

¾ cup Greek-style yogurt
4 anchovy fillets, finely chopped
¼ cup pitted kalamata olives, chopped
3–4 tablespoons olive oil
1 teaspoon sea salt
1½ cups spelt flour or
1½ cups kamut flour
½ teaspoon baking powder

* *White spelt flour is lighter in color and texture than whole-wheat spelt flour as it is more finely milled. Either will work in this recipe.*

Although spelt and kamut are types of wheat, they are more easily digested so are suitable for some wheat-restricted diets. They are also higher in protein than wheat flour and contain slightly less kilojoules.

1 Put the yogurt, anchovies, olives, 1 tablespoon of the oil and the salt in a large bowl and stir to combine. Sift the flour and baking powder together. Gradually add the flour and any bran in the strainer to the yogurt mixture, stirring with a wooden spoon until the mixture starts to form a dough, then using your hands to bring it together.

2 Turn the dough out onto a lightly floured work surface and knead until smooth and elastic, about 2–3 minutes. Lightly oil a large bowl, put the dough in it and spread a little extra oil over the top of the dough to prevent a crust forming. Cover with plastic wrap and set aside for 20 minutes to rest.

3 Divide the dough into 6 equal portions. Roll each portion out on a lightly floured work surface into an oval shape, approximately ¼ inch thick.

4 Heat a large chargrill pan over medium-high heat. Just before cooking, brush each flat bread with some of the remaining oil. Cook the flat breads, one at a time, for 2 minutes each side or until lightly charred and cooked through. Remove, cover loosely with foil and keep warm while you cook the remaining flat breads. Serve as part of a mezze plate.

TIPS You can experiment with the flavors in these flat breads. Try replacing the anchovies or olives with chopped herbs, such as rosemary or thyme, or adding some finely grated Parmesan cheese.
    The best thing about flat breads is they are quick to make and can even be cooked on the barbecue.

Little spiced fruit scrolls

PREPARATION TIME: 20 MINUTES

COOKING TIME: 30 MINUTES

MAKES 10

3 cups spelt flour (see tips)

2 tablespoons baking powder

4½ tablespoons chilled unsalted butter, diced

1 cup milk

1½ tablespoons unsalted butter, melted

¼ cup firmly packed light brown sugar

2 teaspoons ground cinnamon

1 cup fruit medley (see tips)

1 teaspoon natural vanilla extract

3 tablespoons apricot preserves, warmed

> *These scrolls can be made in minutes, unlike traditional yeast bread. Their only downside is that they do not keep as well. The slightly nutty and mellow flavor of the spelt flour is delicious with spices such as cinnamon and the sweetness of dried fruit and brown sugar.*

1 Preheat the oven to 350°F. Brush a 8 x 12 inch baking tin with melted butter.

2 Sift the flour, baking powder and a large pinch of salt into a large bowl. Use your fingertips to rub in the butter until the mixture resembles coarse crumbs. Make a well in the center, add the milk and mix with a flat-bladed knife, using a cutting action, until the mixture comes together to form a dough.

3 Turn the dough out onto a lightly floured work surface and knead briefly for 1–2 minutes or until smooth. Roll out to a rectangle about 10 x 14 inches and brush the surface with three-quarters of the melted butter. Combine the brown sugar and cinnamon and sprinkle evenly over the melted butter. Combine the dried fruit and vanilla and sprinkle evenly over the sugar mixture.

4 Starting at a long side, roll up the dough like a jelly roll, enclosing the filling. Trim the edges and slice the dough into 10 rounds. Place, cut side up and side by side, in the greased tin and brush the top of each with the remaining melted butter. Bake for 30 minutes or until golden brown. Remove from the oven and set aside for 5 minutes, then brush the top of each scroll with the warm apricot preserves. Eat the scrolls while they are warm.

TIPS You can use white or whole-wheat spelt flour, though whole-wheat spelt flour will give a slightly denser texture.

Fruit medley is a dried fruit blend of sultanas and diced apricots, apples, peaches and pears. You can substitute the same quantity of any diced dried fruit.

These scrolls are best eaten warm on the day they are made. Reheat them in the microwave on medium (50%) for 20 seconds.

Maple & cinnamon spelt granola

PREPARATION TIME: 10 MINUTES
COOKING TIME: 40 MINUTES
MAKES ABOUT 5 CUPS

1½ cups rolled spelt

1½ cups rolled oats

½ cup almonds, chopped

⅓ cup sunflower seeds

¼ cup sesame seeds

1½ teaspoons ground cinnamon

¼ cup pure maple syrup

3 tablespoons firmly packed
light brown sugar

3 tablespoons vegetable oil (such as
sunflower or canola)

2 teaspoons natural vanilla extract

1 cup mixed dried fruit (such as
currants and cranberries)

1 Preheat the oven to 300°F. Put the rolled spelt, oats, almonds, sunflower seeds, sesame seeds and cinnamon in a large bowl and stir to combine. Transfer to a large baking sheet with sides and spread out evenly.

2 Put the maple syrup, sugar and oil in a small saucepan over medium heat and cook, stirring, for 2 minutes or until the sugar has dissolved. Stir through the vanilla. Pour the hot syrup over the spelt mixture and stir until all the ingredients are evenly coated.

3 Bake the granola, stirring every 10 minutes to ensure even browning, for 30–35 minutes or until golden brown and crisp. Remove from the oven, add the dried fruit and stir to combine. Set aside to cool completely.

TIPS You could substitute rolled barley for some of the rolled oats.

It is important to stir the granola every 10 minutes or it will brown unevenly and burn. Cooking it slowly at a low temperature makes it crisp and golden without requiring too much oil or sugar.

Store in an airtight container for up to 1 month.

* Rolled spelt can be used in recipes where you would typically use rolled oats.

Chocolate & date spelt cake

PREPARATION TIME: 30 MINUTES

COOKING TIME: 45–50 MINUTES

SERVES 10–12

½ cup plus 3 tablespoons unsalted butter, softened

1 cup superfine sugar

½ cup firmly packed light brown sugar

1 teaspoon natural vanilla extract

4 eggs, separated

¾ cup white or whole-wheat spelt flour

2 teaspoons baking powder

¼ cup unsweetened cocoa powder, plus extra, to dust

⅔ cup sour cream

⅔ cup chopped dark chocolate, or chocolate chips, melted and cooled

3 oz fresh pitted dates, chopped (about ½ cup)

1 Preheat the oven to 350°F. Grease a round 9½ inch springform cake pan and line the base and sides with parchment paper.

2 Use an electric mixer to beat the butter, sugars and vanilla until light and creamy. Add the egg yolks one at a time, beating well after each addition. Sift the spelt flour, baking powder and cocoa together, then fold into the butter mixture alternately with the sour cream. Stir through the melted chocolate and dates until just combined.

3 Use an electric mixer with a whisk attachment to whisk the egg whites in a clean, dry bowl until firm peaks form. Fold one-third of the egg whites into the chocolate mixture to loosen it, then fold in the remaining egg whites until just combined. Pour into the prepared pan and bake for 45–50 minutes or until firm to touch and there is no underlying wobble.

4 Set aside to cool slightly, then remove the side of the pan and transfer to a wire rack to cool completely. Serve dusted with extra cocoa powder.

TIPS Keep in an airtight container for up to 4 days.

Try serving this indulgent cake with Greek-style yogurt or cream.

* The nutty characteristic of spelt is a perfect match with chocolate and dates in this rich and delicious dessert cake.

Buttermilk spelt flapjacks with honey butter & strawberries

PREPARATION TIME: 20 MINUTES

COOKING TIME: 20 MINUTES

SERVES 4

1½ cups white or whole-wheat spelt flour

1 tablespoon baking powder

3 tablespoons sugar

2 eggs, separated

2 tablespoons unsalted butter, melted, plus extra, for greasing

1 cup buttermilk

1 teaspoon natural vanilla extract

Hulled and halved strawberries, to serve

HONEY BUTTER

6 tablespoons unsalted butter, softened

3 tablespoons honey

* Spelt flour can be substituted in most recipes that contain regular wheat flour. Adding the whisked egg whites separately helps make the flapjacks light and fluffy, even when using whole-wheat spelt flour.

1 To make the honey butter, put the butter and honey in a small bowl and use an electric mixer to beat until pale and fluffy. Set aside.

2 Sift the flour and baking powder into a large mixing bowl. Add the sugar and stir to combine. Make a well in the center, add the egg yolks, melted butter, buttermilk and vanilla and whisk until smooth.

3 Use an electric mixer with a whisk attachment to whisk the egg whites in a clean, dry bowl until firm peaks form. Gently fold the egg whites into the batter until just combined.

4 Heat a large nonstick skillet over medium heat and brush with a little extra melted butter. Pour $\frac{1}{4}$ cup of the batter into the pan and use the back of a spoon to spread the mixture to a circle about 4–5 inches in diameter. Repeat to make another flapjack. Cook for 2 minutes or until bubbles appear on the surface of each. Turn and cook for 1–2 minutes or until cooked through.

5 Transfer the flapjacks to a plate and cover loosely with foil to keep warm. Repeat with the remaining batter, brushing the pan with melted butter before cooking each batch of flapjacks. Serve with strawberries and the whipped honey butter.

TIPS The honey in the honey butter can be replaced with crushed honeycomb, golden syrup or brown sugar.

For a healthier version, omit the honey butter and serve with a dollop of fresh ricotta cheese.

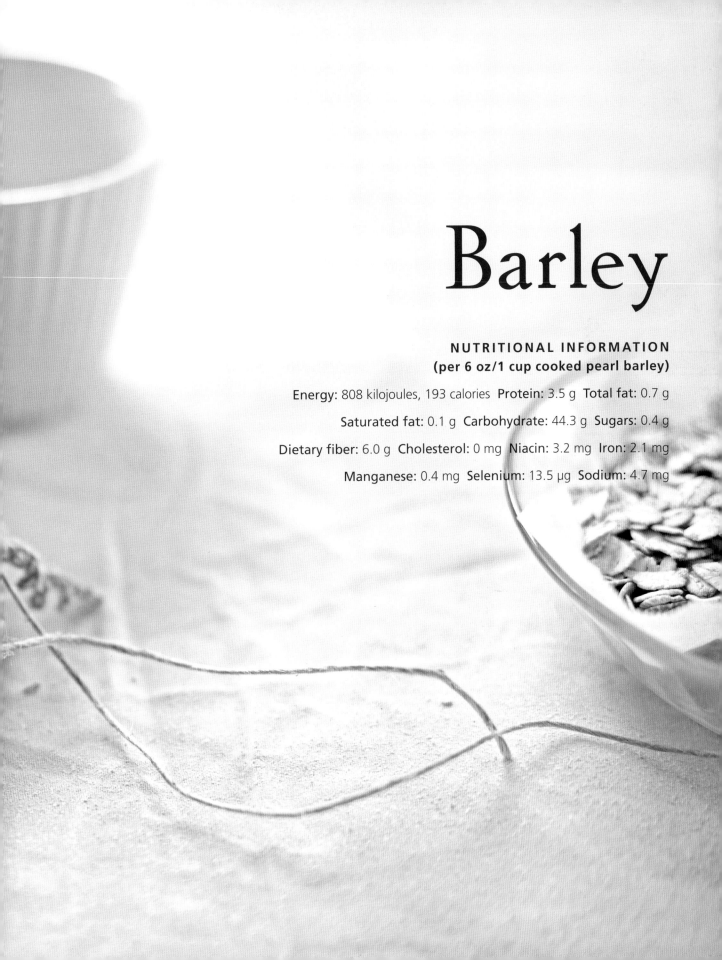

Barley

NUTRITIONAL INFORMATION
(per 6 oz/1 cup cooked pearl barley)

Energy: 808 kilojoules, 193 calories Protein: 3.5 g Total fat: 0.7 g

Saturated fat: 0.1 g Carbohydrate: 44.3 g Sugars: 0.4 g

Dietary fiber: 6.0 g Cholesterol: 0 mg Niacin: 3.2 mg Iron: 2.1 mg

Manganese: 0.4 mg Selenium: 13.5 µg Sodium: 4.7 mg

Barley is a nutritious and versatile grain belonging to the grass family, with a history dating back more than 10,000 years to South-East Asia. During this time, barley was a staple food source for both humans and animals, and it was also used to make alcoholic beverages, as a form of currency and for medicinal purposes (barley water). Barley also played an important role in Greek and Roman culture as it was valued as a nutritious food for athletes and gladiators, and was used in bread making.

Barley looks similar to wheat, although a little paler in color. In medieval Europe, bread made from barley and rye was peasant food, while wheat products were consumed by the upper class. Today, the health benefits of this versatile grain and its delicious nutty flavor are once again being appreciated.

Hulled barley is produced by removing the inedible fibrous outer hull. It is a nutritious and healthy food, but it can be difficult to find. Pearl barley is hulled barley with the bran removed and the grain polished. Pearl barley is less chewy and faster to cook than hulled barley, but is lower in nutrients.

Scotch or pot barley has the outer hull removed by polishing but is less polished and more nutrient dense than pearl barley and is popular in soups, hence its name.

Barley can be processed into a variety of products including flour, flakes similar to oatmeal, and grits. Sprouted barley is naturally high in maltose, a sugar that serves as the basis for both malt syrup and, when fermented, beer and other alcoholic beverages.

Barley is a great food for those with type 2 diabetes or those on a low-GI diet as it has a GI of just 25. Its high soluble-fiber content works in slowing down the absorption of sugar, lowering the overall GI value of a meal.

Barley is packed with beta-glucan soluble fiber, and is therefore linked to a reduced risk of heart disease.

It also contains insoluble fiber, which helps maintain a healthy bowel and can help reduce the risk of cancers such as colon cancer.

Barley is a very good source of selenium, and a good source of phosphorus, copper and manganese. It also contains various phytochemicals including lignans, phenolic acids, phytic acid, plant sterols and saponins.

Pearl barley is by far the most common and readily available form of barley. It is delicious used in salads instead of rice, and has a slightly chewy texture and nutty taste. A winter soup is not quite the same without barley, and it also works beautifully in slow-cooked casseroles and stews. Barley can replace rice in baked desserts, but you do need to cook the barley first to reduce the overall cooking time. It also makes a great risotto that does not require constant stirring.

Barley is also available in flakes, which look similar to rolled oats. These can be used in porridge, crumbles and cookies to name a few. Barley flour can be added to unleavened baked goods such as bread.

To cook barley

Add 1 cup pearl barley to 6 cups boiling water and gently boil for 30 minutes or until *al dente*. Refresh under cold running water, then drain well. If using hulled or pot barley, increase the cooking time to 50–60 minutes.

NOTE Some people like to presoak barley, especially hulled or pot barley, to reduce cooking times. If you are using pearl barley this is not really necessary.

Poached chicken, barley, mint, zucchini & pine nut salad

PREPARATION TIME: 20 MINUTES
COOKING TIME: 45 MINUTES
SERVES 4

1 cup pearl barley, briefly rinsed
1 medium yellow onion, halved
6 black peppercorns
1 teaspoon sea salt
1 lb skinless boneless chicken breasts
2 large zucchini, trimmed
4 baby pattypan squash, trimmed
½ cup mint leaves
3 tablespoons snipped chives
⅓ cup pine nuts, lightly toasted
3 tablespoons dried currants

DRESSING
3 tablespoons olive oil
1½ tablespoons raspberry vinegar
3 tablespoons apple juice

1 Cook the barley in a saucepan of boiling water for 30 minutes or until *al dente*. Refresh under cold running water, then drain well and transfer to a large mixing bowl.

2 Meanwhile, put the onion, peppercorns and salt in a large saucepan with 4 cups water and bring to the boil over high heat. Add the chicken, reduce the heat to low, cover and simmer gently for 5 minutes. Remove from the heat and leave the chicken in the poaching liquid, covered, for 30 minutes. Remove the chicken and discard the liquid. Set aside to cool, then shred.

3 Using a peeler or mandoline, cut the zucchini and squash into thin ribbons. Place in a heatproof bowl, cover with boiling water and set aside for 1 minute. Refresh under cold running water, then drain well.

4 Add the shredded chicken, zucchini, squash, herbs, pine nuts and currants to the bowl with the barley and stir to combine.

5 To make the dressing, put all the ingredients in a small bowl and whisk to combine. Add to the salad and gently toss to combine. Season with sea salt and freshly ground black pepper, to taste.

TIP Zucchini and squash do not need much cooking, and are delicious raw in fact. Blanching them in boiling water maintains their texture, so they give flavor and a slight crunch to salads.

Pearl barley has the lowest GI value of the 'true' grains (i.e. excluding the pseudo-grains) at just 25. Its high-soluble fiber content helps slow down the absorption of sugar, lowering the overall GI value of a meal.

Barley & mushroom ragout with broiled chicken

PREPARATION TIME: 20 MINUTES

COOKING TIME: 1 HOUR

SERVES 4

3 tablespoons olive oil

1½ tablespoons unsalted butter

6 oz (1²/₃ cups) cremini mushrooms, sliced

6 oz (1²/₃ cups) white button mushrooms, sliced

1 large leek, trimmed, halved lengthways and thinly sliced

2 celery ribs, trimmed and diced

2 cloves garlic, crushed

2 teaspoons chopped thyme

1 cup pearl barley, briefly rinsed

½ cup white wine

4 cups chicken or vegetable broth

8 chicken tenderloins or 4 x 6–7 oz boneless chicken breasts, sliced

3 tablespoons sour cream (optional)

Snipped chives, to garnish (optional)

Green salad, to serve

✻ Barley works wonderfully in ragout and risotto. If using presoaked barley, cook for 20–25 minutes and reduce the broth by 1 cup.

1 Heat half the olive oil and the butter in a large heavy-bottomed saucepan over high heat. Add the mushrooms and cook, stirring occasionally, for 5 minutes or until golden. Transfer to a plate and set aside.

2 Return the pan to medium heat, add the remaining oil and cook the leek and celery, stirring occasionally, for 5–6 minutes or until soft. Add the garlic and thyme and cook, stirring, for 1 minute more.

3 Add the barley to the pan and stir to coat the grains in the oil. Add the wine and simmer until it has reduced by half. Add the broth and bring to the boil, then reduce the heat to low, cover and simmer, stirring occasionally, for 30 minutes. Add the mushrooms and stir to combine, then cover and simmer for a further 10–15 minutes or until the barley is tender and creamy and the broth has been absorbed.

4 Meanwhile, heat a large nonstick skillet over high heat and spray with olive oil. Cook the chicken pieces for 3 minutes each side or until golden and cooked through.

5 Stir the sour cream through the ragout, if desired, and season with sea salt and freshly ground black pepper, to taste. Divide the ragout among 4 serving plates or bowls, top with the chicken and garnish with chives, if desired. Serve immediately with a large green salad.

TIPS Any combination of mushrooms can be used, such as oyster, portobello and so on. Browning the mushrooms first, then adding them towards the end of the cooking time means they won't become too soft.

Serving this ragout with a green salad adds more vegetables and also balances the richness of the dish.

Slow-cooked lamb shank & barley soup with gremolata

PREPARATION TIME: 30 MINUTES
COOKING TIME: 2 HOURS 20 MINUTES
SERVES 4–6

3 tablespoons olive oil

4 small lamb shanks, french trimmed

4 oz sliced pancetta,
rind removed, diced

2 medium carrots, peeled and diced

2 celery ribs, trimmed and diced

1 large yellow onion, finely chopped

2 cloves garlic, crushed

2 teaspoons finely chopped rosemary

4 cups chicken broth

1 can (14 oz) chopped tomatoes

1/3 cup pearl barley, briefly rinsed

2 fresh bay leaves

GREMOLATA

1/4 cup chopped flat-leaf parsley

2 teaspoons finely grated lemon zest

1 clove garlic, crushed

1 Heat half the oil in a stockpot or large saucepan over medium-high heat. Add the lamb and cook, turning, for 4–5 minutes or until well browned. Transfer to a plate.

2 Heat the remaining oil in the stockpot. Add the pancetta, carrots, celery and onion and cook, stirring, for 8 minutes or until soft. Add the garlic and rosemary and cook for 1 minute more, then return the lamb to the stockpot.

3 Add the broth, tomatoes, pearl barley and bay leaves to the stockpot. Cover and bring to the boil, then reduce the heat to low and simmer, covered, for 2 hours or until the meat falls from the bones. Use tongs to transfer the lamb to a plate. Remove the meat from the bones and coarsely shred. Skim and discard any excess fat from the surface of the soup, then add the shredded meat and season with sea salt and freshly ground black pepper, to taste.

4 To make the gremolata, combine all the ingredients in a small bowl. Serve the soup sprinkled with gremolata and accompanied by crusty bread.

TIPS This soup can be frozen for up to 2 months. Allow it to cool, then divide among containers, cover with airtight lids and freeze.

If you leave the soup to cool in the refrigerator overnight before shredding the lamb, the fat will solidify on top of the soup and it will be easier to remove.

* *Pearl barley makes a great addition to winter soups, adding flavor and texture as well as dietary fiber. The low-GI content of barley means it will release energy slowly, leaving you feeling fuller for longer.*

Barley, tofu & spinach salad with miso dressing

1½ tablespoons olive oil

2 teaspoons finely grated ginger

1 clove garlic, crushed

1 cup pearl barley, briefly rinsed

2 cups chicken or vegetable broth

1 bunch asparagus (about 5 oz), trimmed, halved lengthways and cut into 1¼ inch lengths

7 oz marinated firm tofu (approx. ½ a package), sliced

1 firm ripe small avocado, halved, pit removed, peeled and sliced (see tips)

Approx 2 cups (4 oz) baby spinach leaves

1½ tablespoons sesame seeds, lightly toasted

MISO DRESSING

3 tablespoons white or yellow (brown) miso paste

3 tablespoons mirin (Japanese cooking wine)

2 tablespoons tamari

1½ tablespoons rice wine vinegar

½ teaspoon sugar

* This salad makes a balanced meal for vegetarians as it combines barley with tofu and sesame seeds, which are both great sources of protein.

1 Heat the olive oil in a large saucepan over medium heat, add the ginger and garlic and cook, stirring, for 30 seconds. Add the barley and cook, stirring, for 2 minutes, then add the broth and 2 cups water and bring to the boil. Reduce the heat to low and simmer for 25 minutes or until *al dente*. Rinse under cold running water, then drain well and transfer to a large mixing bowl.

2 Meanwhile, blanch the asparagus in a saucepan of boiling water until bright green and tender-crisp. Refresh under cold running water, then drain well.

3 To make the miso dressing, put all the ingredients in a small bowl and stir to combine.

4 Add the asparagus, tofu, avocado, baby spinach and half the dressing to the barley and gently toss to combine. Divide the salad among serving bowls, drizzle with a little of the remaining dressing and sprinkle with the sesame seeds.

TIPS Squeeze a little lemon juice over the sliced avocado to prevent it discoloring.

Pearl barley works beautifully with the earthy flavors of miso and tamari. Toasting the barley before cooking, and adding ginger and garlic to the cooking liquid, give lots of additional flavor.

PORK, TOMATO, PAPRIKA
& BARLEY STEW (PAGE 194)

Pork, tomato, paprika & barley stew

PREPARATION TIME: 20 MINUTES
COOKING TIME: 2 HOURS 15 MINUTES
SERVES 4

3 tablespoons olive oil

1½–2 lb trimmed and diced pork shoulder

1 large red onion, diced

2 celery ribs, trimmed and diced

4 oz speck (see tips), diced

2 cloves garlic, thinly sliced

2 teaspoons hot smoked paprika

2 thyme sprigs

¼ cup Spanish sherry

1½ tablespoons concentrated tomato purée

1 can (14 oz) chopped tomatoes

⅓ cup pearl barley, briefly rinsed

1 cup chicken broth

1 teaspoon honey

Arugula and crusty bread, to serve

GREEN OLIVE RELISH

½ cup green olives, pitted and sliced

3 tablespoons chopped flat-leaf parsley

1 Preheat the oven to 325°F. Heat half the oil in a large flameproof casserole dish over high heat and cook the pork, in batches, stirring, for 3–4 minutes or until browned. Transfer to a bowl.

2 Add the remaining oil to the casserole dish and cook the onion, celery and speck, stirring, for 5 minutes or until softened. Add the garlic, paprika and thyme and cook, stirring, for 1 minute more. Add the sherry and simmer until it has almost evaporated, then add the tomato purée and cook, stirring, for 1 minute. Add the tomatoes, barley and broth and stir to combine, then bring to the boil.

3 Return the pork to the casserole dish and stir to coat in the tomato mixture. Cover with a lid or foil and bake for 2 hours or until the pork is very tender. Stir through the honey and season with sea salt and freshly ground black pepper, to taste.

4 Meanwhile, to make the green olive relish, combine the olives and parsley in a small bowl.

5 Divide the stew among serving plates, sprinkle with the relish and serve with arugula and crusty bread.

TIPS You can substitute bacon or pancetta for the speck.
    This stew can be frozen for up to 2 months. Allow it to cool, then divide among airtight containers, cover with the lids and freeze.

✻ *I love adding pearl barley to stews such as this, as it provides body and texture and reduces the amount of meat needed. Serve it with bread to mop up the sauce.*

Barley & oat porridge with fig & hazelnuts

PREPARATION TIME: 5 MINUTES
COOKING TIME: 10 MINUTES
SERVES 4

1 cup rolled oats

1 cup rolled barley

¼ cup chopped dried dessert figs

2 cups milk

⅓ cup hazelnuts, lightly toasted, skinned and chopped

Honey, to drizzle

1 Put the oats, barley, figs, milk and $1\frac{1}{2}$ cups water in a large saucepan. Bring to the boil over high heat, stirring occasionally, then reduce the heat to low and simmer, stirring, for 5 minutes or until thick and creamy.

2 Divide the porridge among 4 serving bowls, top with chopped hazelnuts and a drizzle of honey, and serve.

TIP You can use any combination of dried fruit and nuts in this porridge, such as dried apricots, currants, dates, walnuts, almonds and/or pistachios.

Rolled barley makes a deliciously nutty porridge. I find using equal quantities of barley and oats gives the best result. Barley is packed with beta-glucan soluble fiber and is therefore linked to reduced risk of heart disease.

Baked barley desserts with port-poached prunes

PREPARATION TIME: 15 MINUTES
COOKING TIME: 30 MINUTES
SERVES 4

1 cup cooked pearl barley
(see page 183)

2 eggs

1½ cups milk

3 tablespoons sugar

1 teaspoon natural vanilla extract

½ teaspoon ground nutmeg,
to sprinkle

POACHED PRUNES

4 oz (½ cups) pitted dried prunes,
quartered

3 tablespoons light brown sugar

3 tablespoons port

1 Preheat the oven to 325°F. Lightly grease four ⅔-cup ovenproof ramekins and place on a large baking sheet.

2 Divide the barley evenly among the greased ramekins. Whisk the eggs, milk, sugar and vanilla until well combined, then pour evenly over the barley. Sprinkle the top of each dessert with a little nutmeg and bake for 30 minutes or until puffed and just set (the desserts should have a slight wobble in the center). Set aside to cool slightly.

3 Meanwhile, to make the poached prunes, put all the ingredients in a medium saucepan with ½ cup water and cook over medium heat, stirring to dissolve the sugar. Bring to the boil, then reduce the heat to low and simmer for 5 minutes or until the prunes are syrupy. Remove from the heat and allow to cool a little.

4 Serve the desserts topped with the poached prunes.

TIP These desserts can be served warm or chilled.

※ *Pearl barley can be used as a substitute for short-grain rice in baked desserts. I find cooking the pearl barley first and then baking it in the oven is easier and faster than cooking it on the stovetop.*

In comparison to white-rice desserts, these barley desserts are higher in fiber and protein.

Lemon barley water

PREPARATION TIME: 5 MINUTES

COOKING TIME: 15 MINUTES

MAKES 5 CUPS

½ cup pearl barley

2 lemons, plus lemon slices, extra, to serve

½ cup sugar

> ✳ *Barley water is an ancient home remedy that was given to the sick for ailments such as stomach upsets, cystitis, coughs and colds, to name but a few.*

1 Put the barley in a sieve and rinse under cold running water until the water runs clear. Use a vegetable peeler to remove the lemon zest from the lemons, then juice the lemons.

2 Put the barley, lemon zest and 6 cups water in a large saucepan and bring to the boil, then reduce the heat to low and simmer for 10 minutes. Strain, discarding the barley and zest.

3 Add the sugar to the barley liquid and stir to dissolve, then stir through the lemon juice. Pour the barley water into a bottle/bottles, seal and chill overnight. Serve with lemon slices.

TIPS Although it is traditionally served undiluted, barley water makes a beautifully refreshing drink topped with ice, lemon slices and sparkling mineral water. It is also delicious served with vodka or gin for a summer cocktail.

Keep in the refrigerator for up to 1 week.

Roasted nectarines with barley & almond crumble

PREPARATION TIME: 15 MINUTES
COOKING TIME: 20 MINUTES
SERVES 4–6

6 firm ripe medium nectarines, halved and pits removed

½ cup rolled barley

⅓ cup firmly packed light brown sugar

¼ cup all-purpose flour

1 teaspoon ground cinnamon

⅓ cup sliced almonds

¼ cup unsalted butter, chilled and diced

Vanilla ice cream, plain yogurt or cream, to serve

1 Preheat the oven to 350°F. Lightly grease a 4-cup ovenproof baking dish. Arrange the nectarines, cut side up, in a single layer in the greased dish.

2 Put the barley, sugar, flour, cinnamon and almonds in a medium bowl. Use clean fingertips to rub in the butter until small clumps form. Sprinkle the crumble mixture evenly over the nectarines.

3 Roast the nectarines for 20 minutes or until the crumble is golden and the nectarines are tender. Serve with vanilla ice cream, plain yogurt or cream.

TIP You can replace the nectarines with other seasonal stone fruit, such as plums or peaches.

* Rolled barley can be used in recipes where you would typically used rolled oats, such as here. Rolled barley tends to be slightly firmer than rolled oats, so it makes a lovely crisp topping.

Farro & Freekeh

NUTRITIONAL INFORMATION
(per 3 oz/½ cup uncooked cracked farro)

Energy: 1397 kilojoules, 332 calories Protein: 12.9 g

Total fat: 1.9 g Saturated fat: <1 g Carbohydrate: 52.2 g

Sugars: <1 g Dietary fiber: 4.6 g Sodium: <1 g

NUTRITIONAL INFORMATION
(per 4 oz/½ cup uncooked whole-grain freekeh)

Energy: 1471 kilojoules, 350 calories Protein: 12.6 g Total fat: 2.7 g

Carbohydrate: 72 g Dietary fiber: up to 16.5 g Iron: 4.5 mg

Calcium: 53 mg Magnesium: 110 mg Sodium: 6 mg

Farro (emmer wheat) is an ancient grain, thought
to predate all others, that fed the people of the Near East
and Mediterranean for thousands of years. Ground into
a paste and cooked, it was the primary ingredient in puls,
the polenta eaten by the Roman poor. It sustained Roman
legions and gave rise to the Italian name of flour.

Today farro is mainly grown as a speciality crop in
Italy and a few surrounding countries, but its popularity
extends well beyond those borders as health-conscious
cooks are discovering its appeal.

Farro is rich in fiber, protein, magnesium, niacin and
zinc, as well as phytonutrients and antioxidants including
lignans, phenolic acids, phytic acid, plant sterols and
saponins. As with most varieties of wheat, farro/emmer is
unsuitable for sufferers of wheat allergies or celiac disease.
But it is gentler on the digestive system than common
wheat as the gluten molecules are not as strong.

Farro is sold as the whole grain or cracked farro.
Whole-grain farro takes 50–60 minutes to cook, so is
often soaked overnight prior to cooking to reduce this
time to 25–30 minutes. Cracked farro (traditionally known
as *farro spezzato*) is where the farro grains have been split
during the milling process — it requires less cooking time
(about 20 minutes) and doesn't need presoaking.

Farro is delicious added to stews, casseroles, hearty
soups such as minestrone, or used as a salad grain. It can
also be ground to make flour and can then be used in
pasta and bread making. Try using farro in recipes that
traditionally use pearl barley or spelt.

There is often confusion between farro (emmer)
and spelt, and while closely related and similar in many
features, they are not always interchangeable in recipes.

To cook farro

WHOLE GRAIN Add 1 cup farro to 6 cups boiling water.
Return to the boil, then reduce the heat, cover and simmer
for 50 minutes or until the grains are *al dente*. Rinse under
cold running water, then drain well. If farro has been
presoaked, reduce the cooking time to 20–30 minutes.

CRACKED Add 1 cup cracked farro to 6 cups boiling
water. Return to the boil, then reduce the heat, cover and
simmer for 15–20 minutes or until the grains are *al dente*.
Rinse under cold running water, then drain well.

Freekeh (pronounced free-ka) is wheat that
is picked while green and then put through a roasting
process. It dates as far back as the 1200s and is popular in
Middle Eastern and North African cuisines.

Freekeh is becoming more readily available, as the
nutritional benefits of green wheat have been discovered.
Compared to regular wheat, freekeh contains higher levels
of protein and dietary fiber, as well as various vitamins
and minerals including calcium, potassium, iron and zinc.
Whole-grain freekeh has a GI of 43, so it's a great food
for diabetics and those on a low-GI diet.

It is available in its whole-grain form or as cracked
freekeh, where the grains are cracked during the milling
process. Both whole-grain and cracked freekeh are
delicious in salads such as tabouleh, and work beautifully
with Middle Eastern flavors and spices. They can also
be added to soups and stews or used as stuffings.

To cook freekeh

WHOLE GRAIN Add 1 cup freekeh to 6–8 cups boiling
water. Return to the boil, then reduce the heat, cover and
simmer for 45–50 minutes or until the grains are *al dente*.
Rinse under cold running water, then drain well.

CRACKED Add 1 cup cracked freekeh to 6–8 cups boiling
water. Return to the boil, then reduce the heat, cover and
simmer for 15 minutes or until the grains are *al dente*.
Rinse under cold running water, then drain well.

Farro minestrone

PREPARATION TIME: 20 MINUTES

COOKING TIME: 1 HOUR

SERVES 4

3 tablespoons olive oil

4 oz pancetta, rind removed, diced

1 large yellow onion, finely chopped

2 medium carrots, peeled and diced

2 celery ribs, trimmed and diced

1 medium zucchini, trimmed and diced

3 cloves garlic, crushed

1 teaspoon thyme leaves

3 tablespoons concentrated tomato purée

2 inch piece Parmesan cheese rind

¾ cup cracked farro

1 can (14 oz) chopped tomatoes

5 cups chicken broth

4 cups (½ lb) kale, trimmed, shredded (see tips)

Grated Parmesan cheese, chopped parsley and crusty bread, to serve

1 Heat the oil in a large saucepan over medium heat. Add the pancetta, onion, carrots, celery and zucchini and cook, stirring occasionally, for 7–8 minutes or until the vegetables are soft. Add the garlic and thyme and cook, stirring, for 1 minute. Add the tomato purée and cook, stirring, for 1 minute more.

2 Stir in the Parmesan rind, farro, tomatoes and broth and bring to the boil. Reduce the heat to low and simmer, stirring occasionally, for 45 minutes or until the soup has thickened. Add the kale and simmer for a further 5 minutes.

3 Season with sea salt and freshly ground black pepper, to taste. Add a little extra water if the soup has become too thick. Remove the Parmesan rind. Ladle the soup into serving bowls, sprinkle with the grated Parmesan and parsley and serve with crusty bread.

TIPS Kale is also sold as Tuscan, dinosaur or black kale, or as cavolo nero. Remove and discard the stalks before shredding the leaves.

This soup can be frozen for up to 2 months. Allow to cool, then divide among airtight containers, cover with the lids and freeze.

✳ Farro is similar to pearl barley once cooked, so it works well in soups. Compared to regular wheat, it is higher in fiber, protein, zinc and B vitamins.

If kale is not available, you can substitute swiss chard or English spinach.

Roasted bell pepper & freekeh salad with labne

PREPARATION TIME: 20 MINUTES
COOKING TIME: 45 MINUTES
SERVES 4

1 cup freekeh

2 large red bell peppers, halved and seeded

1 can (14 oz) chickpeas, drained and rinsed

3 tablespoons snipped chives

3 oz (2 cups) baby arugula

5 oz labne (see tip)

DRESSING

2 tablespoons olive oil

2 tablespoons lemon juice

1 teaspoon sumac, plus extra, to serve

2 teaspoons honey

1 Cook the freekeh in a large saucepan of lightly salted boiling water for 45 minutes or until tender. Rinse under cold running water, then drain well.

2 Meanwhile, preheat the broiler on high. Place the bell peppers, skin side up, on a baking sheet and broil until the skin is blistered, about 6–8 minutes. Transfer to a heatproof bowl and cover with plastic wrap. Set aside to cool slightly, then carefully peel away and discard the skin and thinly slice the flesh. Set aside.

3 To make the dressing, whisk together the olive oil, lemon juice, sumac and honey.

4 Put the cooked freekeh, bell peppers, chickpeas, chives and arugula in a large bowl. Add the dressing and gently toss to combine, then season with salt and pepper, to taste. Serve topped with the labne and sprinkled with a little extra sumac.

TIP Labne is yogurt cheese made from strained plain yogurt. It has a tangy taste and creamy texture. If you are unable to find it you can substitute marinated feta cheese.

* Freekeh is wheat that is picked while young and the grain is green. It is higher in nutrients such as protein, fiber, calcium, iron and zinc, than mature wheat. Freekeh has over five times as much fiber and twice as much protein as white rice.

Both whole-grain and cracked freekeh are ideal to use in salads where you would typically use rice or couscous.

Oxtail & farro ragù

PREPARATION TIME: 30 MINUTES
COOKING TIME: 3 HOURS 30 MINUTES
SERVES 4–6

¼ cup all-purpose flour

2½–3 lb oxtail pieces

3 tablespoons olive oil

2 large yellow onions, finely chopped

2 large carrots, peeled and diced

2 celery ribs, trimmed and diced

5 oz back bacon or Canadian bacon, rind removed and diced

3 cloves garlic, thinly sliced

3 anchovy fillets, chopped

2 teaspoons chopped rosemary

3 tablespoons concentrated tomato purée

2 cups red wine

2 cups beef broth

½ cup cracked farro

Whole-wheat spaghetti, to serve

Finely grated Parmesan cheese, to garnish

1 Preheat the oven to 325°F. Place the flour on a large plate and season with sea salt and freshly ground black pepper. Toss the oxtail in the seasoned flour, shaking off any excess. Heat half the oil in a large flameproof casserole dish and brown the oxtail, in batches, for 2–3 minutes. Transfer to a bowl and set aside.

2 Return the dish to medium heat and add the remaining oil, the onions, carrots, celery and bacon. Cook, stirring occasionally, for 6–7 minutes or until the vegetables have softened. Add the garlic, anchovies and rosemary and cook, stirring, for 1 minute more.

3 Add the tomato purée and cook, stirring, for 1 minute. Add the wine and simmer for 2 minutes, then add the broth and 1 cup water and bring to the boil. Return the oxtail to the dish, cover and bake for 2 hours. Stir in the farro, then cover and bake for a further 1 hour or until the meat is tender and falling off the bone. Remove from the oven and set aside to cool slightly.

4 Use tongs to transfer the oxtail to a plate. Remove the meat from the bones and coarsely shred. Skim any excess fat from the surface of the ragù. Return the shredded meat to the casserole dish and season with sea salt and freshly ground black pepper, to taste.

5 Serve the ragù tossed with spaghetti and garnished with Parmesan.

TIP You could also serve this ragù with mashed potato or soft polenta. I also like to serve it with a salad, to make it a more complete meal and balance the richness of the ragù.

The farro's role in this ragù is threefold: it gives texture to complement the softness of the oxtail, it thickens the braising liquid and it helps cut through the richness of the meat. Farro makes a good addition to soups and stews, and is rich in protein, fiber, zinc and B vitamins.

SLOW-ROASTED LAMB
SALAD WITH FREEKEH &
POMEGRANATE (PAGE 214)

Slow-roasted lamb salad with freekeh & pomegranate

PREPARATION TIME: 25 MINUTES
COOKING TIME: 3 HOURS–3 HOURS
30 MINUTES
SERVES 4

1 teaspoon cumin seeds

½ teaspoon ground cinnamon

2½–3 lb boneless lamb shoulder

1½ tablespoons olive oil, plus
2 tablespoons, extra

¼ cup pomegranate molasses (see tip),
plus 1½ tablespoons, extra

1½ tablespoons honey

1 cup cracked freekeh

2 bunches broccolini (about 1 lb
in total), trimmed and cut into
long florets

½ small red onion, thinly sliced

1 pomegranate, seeds removed
and juice reserved

You can use whole-grain freekeh in this recipe, but it will take 45 minutes to cook.

Unlike mature wheat, freekeh is rich in lutein and zeaxanthin, which are linked to the prevention of macular degeneration.

1 Preheat the oven to 325°F. Crush the cumin seeds and cinnamon in a mortar and pestle. Drizzle the lamb with the oil and rub with the crushed spices, then season well with sea salt and freshly ground black pepper. Brown the lamb in a large nonstick skillet over medium-high heat, turning to brown both sides.

2 Place the lamb shoulder in a large roasting pan and brush with about three-quarters of the combined pomegranate molasses and honey. Place a large piece of parchment paper over the lamb, tucking the edges under, then cover the entire pan with a layer of foil. Roast the lamb for 2½–3 hours or until the meat is extremely tender and can be shredded with a fork. Brush the remaining pomegranate mixture over the lamb, then set aside to cool slightly. Coarsely shred the meat.

3 Meanwhile, cook the freekeh in a large saucepan of lightly salted boiling water for 15–20 minutes or until *al dente*. Rinse under cold running water, then drain well, squeezing out as much excess water as possible. Transfer to a large bowl.

4 Blanch the broccolini in a large saucepan of boiling water until bright green and tender-crisp. Refresh under cold running water, then drain well. Add the broccolini, onion and three-quarters of the pomegranate seeds to the freekeh and stir to combine.

5 Whisk together the extra olive oil and pomegranate molasses and 1 tablespoon of the reserved pomegranate juice. Add to the salad and toss to combine, then season with salt and pepper, to taste.

6 To serve, pile the salad onto a large serving platter, top with the shredded lamb and sprinkle with the remaining pomegranate seeds.

TIP Pomegranate molasses is made from reduced pomegranate juice and has a rich sweet-and-sour taste, similar to tamarind. It is available from speciality food stores and Middle Eastern delicatessens. You can substitute 2 teaspoons tamarind pulp or 3 tablespoons lemon juice.

Red wine farro risotto

PREPARATION TIME: 15 MINUTES

COOKING TIME: 50 MINUTES

SERVES 4

4 cups vegetable or chicken broth

1½ tablespoons olive oil

1½ tablespoons butter

1 large red onion, finely chopped

2 cloves garlic, crushed

1½ cups cracked farro

1½ cups red wine

½ cup finely grated Parmesan cheese, plus extra, to serve

Chopped flat-leaf parsley, to serve

1 Bring the broth to the boil in a medium saucepan over high heat, then reduce the heat to very low and keep at a gentle simmer.

2 Heat the olive oil and butter in a large heavy-bottomed saucepan over medium heat. Add the onion and cook, stirring occasionally, for 5 minutes or until soft. Add the garlic and cook, stirring, for 1 minute.

3 Add the farro and cook, stirring, for 1–2 minutes or until evenly coated in the oil mixture. Add 1 cup of the wine and let it bubble away until reduced by half. Start adding the broth, a ladleful at a time, and cook, stirring, until it is absorbed before adding more. When about half the broth is used, add the remaining wine, then continue adding the remaining broth a ladleful at a time.

4 When you have added all the broth and the farro is tender, about 30–35 minutes, remove the risotto from the heat and add the Parmesan. Cover and set aside for 5 minutes. Serve immediately, garnished with parsley and extra Parmesan.

TIP For a really indulgent risotto, add a knob of butter with the Parmesan at the end.

* Farro produces a risotto with a slightly nutty flavor and chewy texture, similar to pearl barley. The earthiness of the farro is well matched with red wine and Parmesan here.

This risotto is quite rich and very filling, so you only need to serve small portions. To make a balanced meal, serve it with a salad of bitter greens, such as Belgian endive, arugula and thinly sliced pear.

Chicken & freekeh tagine with lemon and green olives

PREPARATION TIME: 30 MINUTES
(+ 1 HOUR MARINATING)
COOKING TIME: 1 HOUR 30 MINUTES
SERVES 4

⅓ cup firmly packed cilantro leaves

⅓ cup firmly packed parsley leaves

2 cloves garlic, crushed

1 long red chile, seeded and finely chopped

2 teaspoons ground cumin

1 teaspoon ground turmeric

3 tablespoons lemon juice

3 tablespoons olive oil

3–4 lb chicken pieces on the bone (we used thighs and legs)

1 large red onion, thinly sliced

4 strips lemon zest

2 cups chicken broth

½ cup freekeh

¼ cup pitted dried dates, chopped

½ cup green olives

Arugula leaves, to garnish

1 Put the cilantro, parsley, garlic, chile, cumin, turmeric, lemon juice and half the olive oil in a blender or food processor and blend to a smooth paste, adding 1–2 tablespoons hot water if necessary. Season with sea salt and freshly ground black pepper.

2 Place the chicken pieces in a large shallow glass or ceramic container, add half the marinade (reserve the remaining marinade) and turn to coat. Cover and refrigerate for at least 1 hour.

3 Preheat the oven to 350°F. Heat the remaining oil in a large flameproof casserole dish over high heat. Brown the chicken, in batches, for 2–3 minutes or until golden. Transfer to a bowl and set aside.

4 Return the dish to medium heat, add the onion and cook, stirring occasionally, for 5 minutes or until softened. Add the reserved marinade and cook, stirring, for 1–2 minutes or until fragrant. Return the chicken to the dish with the lemon zest, broth, freekeh and dates and bring to the boil. Cover and bake for 1 hour. Add the olives and bake, covered, for a further 15 minutes or until the freekeh is tender. Skim any fat from the surface. Serve garnished with extra arugula leaves.

TIP You can use a whole chicken, cut into 8 pieces, for this recipe.

* Freekeh works really well in slow-cooked dishes, such as this tagine, and soups. Its herbaceous flavor is delicious with the freshness of lemon, cilantro and parsley. Whole-grain freekeh has a GI of just 43.

Warm farro, pancetta & parsley salad

PREPARATION TIME: 15 MINUTES
COOKING TIME: 30 MINUTES
SERVES 4

1¼ cups cracked farro

5 oz pancetta, rind removed,
cut into lardons

1 shallot, finely chopped

2 celery ribs, trimmed and
cut into ¼ x 2 inch batons

3 tablespoons finely chopped
flat-leaf parsley

RED WINE VINAIGRETTE

3 tablespoons olive oil

2 teaspoons red wine vinegar

1½ tablespoons lemon juice

1 clove garlic, crushed

½ teaspoon honey

1 Cook the farro in a large saucepan of lightly salted boiling water for 15–20 minutes or until *al dente*. Rinse briefly under cold running water, then drain well and transfer to a large bowl.

2 To make the red wine vinaigrette, whisk all the ingredients together in a small bowl.

3 Heat a large, deep skillet over high heat and cook the pancetta, stirring, for 3–4 minutes or until golden. Reduce the heat to medium and add the farro, red wine vinaigrette, shallot, celery and parsley. Season with sea salt and freshly ground black pepper and stir to combine. Cook until heated through, then serve.

TIP This warm salad is delicious served with broiled meat, such as chicken or pork.

* *Farro can be purchased as either whole-grain or cracked. The most readily available is cracked farro and it cooks in about half the time whole-grain requires. If using whole-grain farro, soak it in cold water for several hours before cooking, then simmer in boiling water for up to 1 hour, until* al dente.

Index

Whole grain suppliers

Eden Organic
www.edenfoods.com

Bob's Red Mill
www.bobsredmill.com

Bluebird Grain Farms
www.bluebirdgrainfarms.com

Text © 2013 Murdoch Books
Design © 2013 Murdoch Books
Photography © 2013 Murdoch Books
Cover photography by Julie Renouf

A Second Appetite by Random House edition published 2015

Library and Archives of Canada Cataloguing in Publication is available upon request

ISBN: 178-0-449-01688-6

Recipes, text and styling: Chrissy Freer
Designer: Susanne Geppert
Photographer: Julie Renouf
Project Editor: Martina Vascotto
Editor: Anna Scobie
Food Editor: Christine Osmond
Home Economist: Caroline Griffiths
Production: Karen Small

Printed by Hang Tai Printing Company Limited, China

The Publisher and stylist would like to thank Breville, Country Road, Est Australia, Market Import, Mozi, Mud Australia, Royal Hamam, Status Collections, The Works Bed Bath N' Table and Urban Edge Ceramics for lending equipment and props for use and photography.

IMPORTANT: Those who might be at risk from the effects of salmonella poisoning (the elderly, pregnant women, young children and those suffering from immune deficiency diseases) should consult their doctor with any concerns about eating raw eggs.

OVEN GUIDE: You may find cooking times vary depending on the oven you are using. For convection ovens, as a general rule, set the oven temperature to 35°F (20°C) lower than indicated in the recipe.

Published in Canada by Appetite by Random House, a division of Random House of Canada Limited, a Penguin Random House company.

www.randomhouse.ca

9 8 7 6 5 4 3 2 1